Women Participation in Leadership and Decision Making Positions

Women Participation in Leadership and Decision Making Positions

Dr. Karanam Viswa Bhushan

KALPAZ

First Published, 2021

Published by

Kalpaz Publications
C-30, Satyawati Nagar,
Delhi – 110052
Ph.: 011-47034999, 9811692060
www.kalpazpublications.com
E-mail: kalpaz@hotmail.com

Printed at: Gyan Press, Delhi.

Cataloging in Publication Data—DK
Courtesy: D.K. Agencies (P) Ltd. <docinfo@dkagencies.com>

Bhushan, Karanam Viswa, 1963- **author.**
Women participation in leadership and decision making positions / Dr. Karanam Viswa Bhushan.
pages cm
Includes bibliographical references.
ISBN 9789353246068 (HB)

1. Women—Political activity—Ethiopia—Addis Ababa. 2. Leadership in women—Ethiopia—Addis Ababa. 3. Decision making—Ethiopia—Addis Ababa. I. Title.

LCC HQ1236.5.E8B48 2021 | DDC 320.0820963 23

Contents

Acknowledgements

First and foremost, I would like to express my gratitude from the core of my heart to the Almighty God for his heavenly blessings.

I would like to express my gratitude to my student Tsigewoiny Zekarias who involved in the research work and contributed her efforts and abilities. .

My deepest expression of appreciation and heartfelt thanks to my friend Christine Durocher for their unreserved inspiration and moral support for this book publication

I would like to acknowledge all the participants and contributors of the research work who forwarded their ideas, believes, agreements and disagreements.

My special thanks go to all my sisters and brothers for the generous support and contribution.

List of Tables

List of Figures

Chapter One

Introduction

The aim of this study is to address women's participation in leadership and decision making positions in public institutions of Bole Sub city. In relation to this, the current status of, and factors affecting women's participation in leadership and decision making positions in public institutions of that Sub city was addressed. It has also addressed men's perception and the existing policy, towards women's participation in leadership and decision making position in the same area.

In this paper, participation is defined as the provision of equal opportunity to women to take part in the leadership, decision making and management of the institutions. It implies quantitative and qualitative participation of women in Bole Sub City decision making positions.

1.1. Background of the Study

In recent years it has been widely recognized that women's active participation in decision making positions is central to development and poverty alleviation. The Universal Declaration of Human Rights states that achieving the goal of equal participation of women and men in decision making will provide a balance for the achievement of both transparent and accountable government to strengthen democracy and promote its proper functioning (Afroz, 2010)

Gender empowerment of women refers to women and men being equally entitled to all rights, participation and benefits. Political empowerment also refers to quantitative and qualitative participation of women in public representation and decision making areas at all levels. It includes structural transformation and capacity building as mechanism to empowerment. The basic areas of women empowerment reinforce each other. Women's Political empowerment for instance plays a key role in promoting to political, social and economic interest and participation of women (EC, 2010).

Globally, the political participation of women in political leadership is increasing at a lower rate. At the moment, the global average of women parliamentarians is 19.5 percent. It falls below the 30% target that was to be achieved by 2005. This target was set in the1995 Beijing Platform for Action. Nevertheless, it is worth noting that the percentage of women Parliamentarian has increased. A report by Inter-Parliamentarian Union, 2012 indicates that the global average of female parliamentary representation stood at 19.8 percent in 2011 up from 19 percent in 2010.This 0.8 percentage increase has followed similar patterns over the past decade and underscores the minimal progress it attempts to reach gender parity in parliamentary representation across the globe this century (Inter-Parliamentary Union, 2012).

In Africa, women's political participation has increased in recent years. However, there still exists a gender disparity between men's and women's level of political participation (Sirleaf 2010). It is noted that the share of Parliamentary seats held by women increased from 7 percent in 1990 to 17 percent in 2007 and 20.4% in 2011, which is more than the global average (IPU 2012). The increase in political participation is as a result of constitutional quotas written into law and requiring that certain percentage of political positions to be occupied by women (Pooter, 2009).

According to (Hess C., 2002), participation of women in political life and decision making plays a crucial role in the development of women. He also stated that to achieve development and human rights, there should be equal involvement of women and men in decision making area. The right to equal participation of women in decision making is the most important human and democratic rights of women. Accordingly, equal participation of men and women in all aspects such as political, social and economical decision making positions is imperative.

In recent years it has been widely recognized that women's active participation in decision making is central to development and poverty alleviation. The Universal Declaration of Human Rights states that achieving the goal of equal participation of women and men in decision making will provide a balance for the achievement of both transparent and accountable Government to strengthen democracy and promote its proper functioning (Afroz, 2010)

The national policy on women underscores the critical importance of enhancing gender equality in all spheres of life through gender mainstreaming. The policy also urges sector ministries and organizations to consider gender equality in the planning, implementation, monitoring and evaluation of all activities and program (Takabo H, 2010).

Additionally, Ethiopia ratified different human rights, instruments and policies to achieve equal participation of women in leadership position. Though the government has ratified different policies, regulations and other enhancing instruments, the real participation of women in former organization from the top to down is still insignificant. Moreover, in 1993, Ethiopia, launched a women's policy to facilitate conditions conducive to the speeding of equality between man and woman so that woman could participate politically, socially and economically on equal firms with man, (USAID-IQPEP, 2012)

In addition, the study conducted by (Haregewoin, 2009) indicated that opportunities to participate women in decision making and politics in Ethiopia are at subordinate position when compared with men. Although, they are involved in the social, economic, cultural and political spheres, when they are compared with their male counterparts, they benefit less from their contribution and are less involved in decision making levels. In addition, Ministry of Women Affairs (2004) discussed that the status of women in Ethiopia compared to men, are clearly in a disadvantageous position in all respects. They benefit less from social services and hold inferior positions in all economic, political, social and cultural, affairs. During the 1995 general election for regional council 5.0% were women. Thus in the elector held in 2000 for regional council, there were (12.9%) women, which have shown an increase by 7.9%. Regarding the level of international representation among the 28 ambassadors that Ethiopia appointed at different mission abroad shows only 4 (14.3%) are women (MOWA, 2004). Similar situation is observed in terms of women participation in decision making in some selected public organization, like Bole sub city in Addis Ababa city administration where currently from 38 office head positions 32 are occupied by men while women occupy only 6 office head positions. In the sub city from 65 departments head position 50 are held by men where as only 15 women held this position (2018). This is why I intended to do a research on what factors are affecting women participation in leadership and decision making positions taking the case of Bole sub city.

This research will focus on digging out and diagnosis the existing gender gap in leadership and decision making positions and will come up with some suggestions for overcoming different barriers to represent women's participation in leadership and decision making positions.

1.3. Description of the Study Area (Background of the Study Area)

Bole sub city is one of the ten (10) sub cities of Addis Ababa. It is located in the Eastern part of Addis Ababa City

Bole Sub-City Administration
Area: 122.08 sq.km
Population: 328,900
Male: 154,542
Female: 174,358
Population density per sq. m: 2,694.1
No. of Weredas: 14
Office Location: Megenagna

Source: www.addisababa.gov.et/es/web/guest/bole-sub-city

Map of Addis Ababa City Administration

Administration. It is bordered by Yeka Sub city in the North, Kirkos and Nifas Silk Lafto Sub cities in the West, Akaki Sub city in the South and 'Oromiya Liyu Zone' in the East. It has got an area of 122.08 sq. km. Administratively, it is divided in to 14 Woredas. According to CSA 2008, the sub city has a total population of the 328,900 comprising 174,358 (53%) Female and 154,542 (47%) Male. Regarding the life style, Very poor and very rich people live in the sub city. Various National and International organizations including Embassies live in this sub city. Both Rural and urban dwellers are found in this sub city.

1.4. Statement of the Problem

Ethiopia is developing nation and is among the countries which have high population in Africa, and having almost similar number of women and men in the entire population. Ethiopia is among the most fast growing countries in the world. Therefore, the country needs to use all the human capitals because their contribution to the development of the country is instrumental in all spheres including in political leadership. Unequal representation of women and men results in underdevelopment. This is because the full potential of the country is underutilized. In relation to this idea, UNDP (2002) identified equal participation of women in political life and decision making area plays important role in the improvement of women in terms of their confidence, but exclusive of women from equal participation in leadership and decision making, target of equality, development and human right cannot be attained.

Women's participation in executive organ of the government is very low all over the world.

(Stelter, 2002) adds on this that women are less represented in position of power and decision making compared with that of men, especially, those areas which are found at higher hierarchies are controlled by men. In different areas, women have access to first level or middle level positions in their organizations.

Especially, the culture of Ethiopia is dominated by patriarch. This leads to gender inequality. Due to this, every activity like politics, economic, legal and religious institutions are under the control of men (Azeb, 2003). The author adds on this idea that women's less participation in higher leaderships of positions and also less participated comparing to the other world in Political activity. According to (CSA, 2007), Ethiopian women accounts to **49.5%** of the total population and in AA City Administration Bole sub city is **53%.** In Bole Sub City, there are 269 (153 male and 116 female) representatives in the House of Representatives in Sub city level and 2,860 (1,589 male and 1,271 female) at Woerda level. This shows that the representation of women and men is not in line with their number in the total population. In addition to this, they are less represented in leadership and decision making position and they don't even stay for long time in positions they get, especially at executive level.

In line with this matter, the current situation (2018) of Bole Sub City in Addis Ababa City Administration shows that from 38 positions in the head office, 32 are occupied by men while only 6 are occupied by women. In the same manner, from 65 department head positions in the sub city, 50 and 15 positions are occupied by men and women respectively. Therefore the integration of women at high and middle level leadership position is at subordinate. When compared to men, it shows that, in the head office level only 15.8 % and in department head level only 23% held of the positions is occupied by women. This indicates that women are less represented at leadership positions. So this data indicates that the upper and middle level position in the above selected public institution of the Bole sub city in Addis Ababa city administration are still dominated by men.

The Women and Child Affairs organization has duties and responsibilities to implement women policy, though it does not participate equally women as compared to men leadership position in this sub city and department head positions.

(Meaza, 2009) further noted that Ethiopia is party to all major human right treaties including the most important women's conventions, i.e., CEDAW which calls for equal participation of women in public decision making, Beijing Declaration and platform of Action (BDPA),which requires government to attain a 30% benchmark for women's representation in all public decision making positions (Meaza, 2009) . Moreover, various literatures argue that as compared to prior decades, the participations of women in decision making throughout the world are somehow increasing. But, in spite of the incremental progress towards women's participation in public spheres, it is generally recognized that women have largely remained outside of formal leadership roles due to various factors.

Consequently, the study was aimed to investigate the existing gender gap in decision making and leadership and to identify the major challenges that hinder women's participation in decision-making position. In addition, the study has examined the level of understanding of the importance of encouraging women to decision making, and examining the policy framework that is used to bring women to the decision making position in some selected sectors and Woredas of the sub city.

1.5. Basic Research Questions

The study was sought to address the following research questions.

1. What are the current status of women in leadership and decision making in public organizations of the sub city?
2. What are the attitudes of women and their men counter parts towards women's participation in decision making position in the sub city?
3. How well the existing policy frame work is designed to encourage women participation in leadership and decision making position in the sub city?
4. Which factors (social/cultural factors, organization culture, stereotyping, work place policies, Limited access to advanced education and Discrimination in appointments) significantly contributing to women participations in leadership positions?
5. What are possible solutions for gaps that would be identified?

1.6. Objective of the study

1.6.1. General Objectives

The overall objective of the study is to assess the status of and determine the factors that affect women's participation in leadership and Decision Making Position in public institutions of Bole Sub city.

1.6.2. Specific Objectives

The Specific objectives of this study are to;

- Explore the current status of women's participation in Decision Making Position of the Sub city.
- Assess the awareness and attitudes of women themselves and their men counter parts towards women's participation in Decision Making Position in the sub city.

- Examine how well the existing policy framework is designed to encourage women's participation in leadership and Decision Making Position in the sub city.
- Determine which factor(s) significantly affect the women's participation in leadership and Decision Making Position.
- Generate possible solutions for gap that would be identified from the results of the study.

1.7. Significance of the Study

The finding of this study is expected to provide valuable information to different organs/users at different levels.

- The finding of this research will help the government to enhance women's participation in leadership and decision making position and take corrective action towards women participation in leadership positions in the country in general and in Bole Sub city of Addis Ababa City Administration in particular.
- It will help policy makers to review or redesign strategies to effectively improve the implementation of women's participation in leadership positions in the Sub city.
- It will help women leaders who give information regarding the factors that affect women's participation in leadership positions and empower them to pave the way for other women.
- Moreover, the study will serve as a base for future researchers who may focus on similar and related topics and issues.

1.8. Scope of the Study

1.8.1. Content Scope

This study was delimited on the Factors Affecting Women's Participation in Leadership and decision Making Positions in Addis Ababa City Administration the case of Bole Sub City. The study was conducted through descriptive analytical survey design. The study has also been delimited on the eight selected sectors and three Woredas. The Sectors are Women, Child and Youth, Public Service, Finance and Economic Development, Trade office, Education, Human resource and Social Affairs, Industry development and the Council office of the Sub City where as the Woredas are; Woreda 1, 6 and 12. The reason why these sectors and Woredas were selected is that the required (relevant and reliable) information can be collected. The study was also confined to key government officials, top and middle level managers, experts and employees of the sectors and Weredas under consideration.

1.8.2. Geographical Scope

Geographically, the study was undertaken at Bole Sub city of Addis Ababa City Administration. This Sub city was taken for study for the reason that among the ten Sub cities in Addis Ababa, it is a Sub city where people with different life styles (very rich and very poor) reside together. Among these people, the number of female counts more than half. Besides to this, different national and international organizations including Embassies are found in this sub city.

1.8.3. Time Scope

The problem understudy has existed for years and still exists. Hence, the study has covered the period 2018-2019. This was to study the current situation of the problem and be able to suggest solution for the future.

1.9. Limitation of the Study

In the world of uncertainty, everything is limited to some conditions. Therefore, there were potential threats related to finance, time, transport, availability of data, availability of the respondents, timely response of the respondents, luck of adequate support from concerned bodies and other resource required for the research.

1.10. Definition of Key Terms

Leadership: Before defining leadership it is important to see some concepts of leader. The concept of a leader implies a role relationship of some duration, although this duration is not great or the role so unvarying as is often thought. A leader however, is one who is frequently perceived to perform acts of leading (Freeman, 2001).

Leadership is a process whereby individual influences a group of individuals to achieve a common goal, emphasizing process or transactional event over the traits or characteristics residing in the leader. Leadership is composed task behaviors that focus on goal accomplishment or relationship behaviors that help subordinates or followers feel comfortable with themselves, the situation and each other (Chin, 2007).

Participation: Participation in Social Science refers to different mechanisms for the public to express opinions and ideally exert influences regarding political, economical, management and other social decisions (Ajack, 1992). Since in this regards, women's participation can be expressed as the process by which women are participated to engage in both higher and lower level of leadership and decision making positions in order to make decisions regarding political, economical and other social issues.

Women's Participation in Leadership: Women's Participation in Leadership is a function which is participate at all levels of leadership positions representative of the organization help in integrating the personal goals of the employees with the organizational goals, manager and besides that, theorist and guide follower (Mckinsey, R., & Company, S., 2009).

Gender: the socially ascribed differences between men and women (MOWA, 2004).

Gender Equity: Gender Equity as promotion of equal opportunities and fair treatment for men and women in the personal, social, cultural, political, and economic spheres (MOWA, 2004)

Factor: the researcher uses for those hindering women from public sector leadership activities and those which are promotes women to participate in different leadership activities (MOWA, 2004).

Affirmative Action: Prioritized positive measures such as quotas, to promptly correct the difference, in the case that discriminated groups are placed in extremely unequal conditions to other groups, due to discriminations accumulated in the past. Women's political empowerment refers that equal representation of women in positions of power and decision making and equipping them with non quantifiable aspects of women empowerment (UNDP, 1995).

Process Owner: Those leaders who leads the teams of a particular job which is the leader positions below the bureau heads and deputy bureau heads (Wudealem, 2015).

1.11. Organization of the Study

This study is organized into five chapters: Chapter one is the introduction of the study and it consists of the background to the study, Statement of the problem, Objectives of the study, research questions, significance, delimitations, limitations, and operational definition of terms.

Chapter two is the literature review that supports the study and it comprises of introduction of the chapter's content, then the literature review is presented according to the objectives of the study, the conceptual framework is presented at the end of the chapter.

Chapter three discusses the research methodology and it consists of research design, target population, sampling procedures and sample size, research instruments with their reliability and validity, data collection procedures and analysis, ethical consideration of the study variables.

Chapter four contains data analysis, interpretation and presentation. It starts with the analysis of personal details of the respondents and the rest of the chapters are arranged according to the research questions.

Chapter five contains the summary, conclusions, discussion and recommendation of the findings.

Chapter Two

Literature Review

2.1. Definition of Literature Review

A literature review is a comprehensive summary of previous research on a topic. The literature review surveys scholarly articles, books, and other sources relevant to a particular area of research. The review should enumerate, describe, summarize, objectively evaluate and clarify previous research. It should give a theoretical base for the research and help you (the author) determine the nature of your research. The literature review acknowledges the work of previous researchers, and in so doing, assures the reader that your work has been well conceived. It is assumed that by mentioning a previous work in the field of study, that the author has read, evaluated, and assimilated that work into the work at hand.

2.2. Introduction

The chapter reviewed literature relevant to the study. The sources of literature were text books, magazines, internet, journals, previous research works related to the study. These helped to clarify, strengthen and accordingly direct each stage of research from the formulation of the research topic to the dissemination and utilization of research findings.

In particular relevant literature on factors affecting women's participation in leadership and decision making position (women's upward mobility) was revealed to expose the existing gaps and to offer an insight in to the need for the current study. Finally, a chapter summary was provided . This study sought to investigate the relationship between women's upward mobility (response variables) and the following set of independent variables; social/cultural factor, organizational policies, limited access to advanced education and discrimination of women in appointments.

2.3. Definition and Concept of Important Terms

2.3.1 Definitions and Concept of Participation

According to the (World Bank 1995), cited in (Suad, 2015) the definition of participation as a "process through which stakeholders influence and share control over development initiatives and the decisions and resources which affects them". (John Gaventa and Camilo valderrama, 1999) cited in (Suad, 2015), participation is a joint consultation in decision making, goal setting, profit sharing, teamwork, and other such measures through which affirm attempts to foster or increase its employees commitment to collective objectives.

2.3.2. Definitions and Concept of Decision Making

Nickell, Rice and Tucker (1986) defined, "Decision Making as the process of selecting from alternative courses of action." Acts of choice between alternative courses of action designed to produce a specified result, and one made on a review of relevant information guided by explicit criteria. (Salaman and Thompson 1980)

A conscious and human process involving both individual and social phenomena, based upon factual and value premises, which includes a choice of one behavioral activity from one or more alternatives with the intention of moving towards some desired state of affairs. (Harrison, 1999)

A moment, in an ongoing process of evaluating alternatives for meeting an objective, at which expectations about a particular course of action impel the decision-maker to select that course of action most likely to result in attaining the objective. (Harrison, 1999)

According to the Encyclopedia Dictionary of sociology, "Decision Making is defined as a volitional act resulting in a sequence of actions leading to achievement of a goal through transforming initial information in an uncertain situation. Decision Making is the central process at all levels of data processing and purposeful activity. (Jani, 1999)

In nutshell, decision is not a mechanical job. It is risk taking and a challenge to judgment. The "right answer" is not central. Central is understanding of the problem. Decision Making, further, is not an intellectual exercise. It mobilizes the vision and energies the resources of the organization for effective action.

Further according to Allen (2009), "Management – Decision Making is the work a manager performs to arrive at conclusion and judgment."

Terry (2009), "Decision Making is the selection based on some criteria from two or more possible alternatives."

2.3.3. Meaning and Concept of Leadership

Leadership is process, by which one person influences the thoughts, attitudes, and behaviors of others (Yalem, 2011) Leaders set a direction for the rest of us; they help us see what lies ahead; they help us visualize what we might achieve; they encourage us and inspire us. Leadership is the ability to get other people to do something significant that they might not otherwise do. It's energizing people toward a goal (Yukl, 2006) defines leadership as "*the process of influencing others to understand and agree about what needs to be done and how to do it, as well as the process of facilitating individual and collective efforts to accomplish shared objectives."*

Hence, for this study the definition of leadership as a process of encouraging and helping others to work actively toward objectives is considered since the meaning of leadership is taking into consideration as facilitator (transformational leadership style) not as a power (transactional leadership style).

Early research tried to identify the traits that differed between leaders and non-leaders, or between successful and unsuccessful leaders: Some studies focused on personality factors, like intelligence, ambition, and aggressiveness; others examined physical characteristics like height, build and attractiveness. However, no consistent agreements that are stable across groups and tasks have immerged despite continued attempts (Ibid).

Leadership behavior i.e. the way leaders engage in their activities or perform their role as a leader, and antecedents of behavior has been widely studied. It has been found that personal direction of leaders is associated with pattern of leadership displayed by individuals (Bass and Duntemen as cited in Sikdar & Mitra, 2008).

According to (Sikdar ,Arijit & Mitra Sumit, 2008) leadership literature has identified different styles of leadership based on leader's orientation towards task and people. Transactional leadership behavior is associated with the leader being more tasks oriented and with low consideration towards people. Transactional leadership is characterized by behavior associated more with the "agentic attributes" (i.e. agentic behaviors at work includes speaking assertively, influencing others, and initiating tasks of masculine gender), while transformational leadership behavior is associated with the leader having high consideration of people. It is characterized by behavior focusing on relationship and consideration of people and is associated with the "communal attributes" of feminine gender. Communal behaviors' at work include being concerned with the welfare of others (i.e., descriptions of kindness, sympathy, sensitivity, and nurturance), helping others, accepting others' direction, and maintaining relationships.

This indicating that gender characteristics impact on leadership behavior. Thus it could be influenced by the gender identification i.e. how individuals identify with characteristics attributed to males or females based on gender. People who see themselves as having more feminine characteristics are likely to exhibit the transformational leadership behavior.

2.4. Theoretical Framework

2.4.1. Liberal Feminist Theory

There are several feminist theories that are used in gender studies. They attempt to explain issues involved in decision making, policies and practices of organizations.

In this study, one of the theories used is 'Liberal feminism. Liberal feminism is rooted in the tradition of the 16th and 17th century liberal philosophy. Liberal feminism focused on the ideas of equality and liberty (Wollstonecraft, 1792) as cited in (Brenda, 2015) Mary Wollstonecraft western feminist theorist argued, that women's capacity to reason was equal to that of men and that biological sex differences were irrelevant in granting any rights (Ibid). She further argued that the reason women appeared to be intellectually inferior was due to their inferior education and therefore, was a result of inequality, rather than justification for it.

Liberal feminist see women subordination as resulting from gendered norms, rather than biological sex, and aim to change these norms. Liberal feminists focus on equal opportunities for men and women in education and all sphere of life. The same education provided to a man if provided to a woman will allow a woman to assume responsibility for her own development and growth. But unless society provides equal education with the same civil liberties and economic opportunities a man has, a woman will only exercise her hard won autonomy only within the private or domestic realm. These feminists are also concerned with ensuring that laws and policies do not discriminate against women. Liberal feminists are further looking forward to the removal of barriers that prevent women from operating effectively in public spheres on equal terms with men.

Despite the fact that several policies on affirmative action are in place, women are still lagging behind in all aspects. In Bole sub city for example, though women are employed, very few women are in senior management positions but are concentrated in technical and support staff positions only.

2.4.2. Behavioral theory of leadership

This study was also guided by behavioral theory of leadership. This theory is based on the belief that great leaders are made, not born People can learn to become leaders through teaching and observation. It is rooted in behaviorism, which emphasizes that behaviors can be studied in a systematic and observable manner with no consideration of internal mental states. The proponents of behaviorism theory are Ivan Pavlov, B.F. Skinner, Edward Thorndike, John B. Watson and Clark Hull. This theory focus on how leaders behave. For instance do leaders dictates what need to be done and expect cooperation. On the other hand, do they involve teams in decision making to encourage acceptance and support?

In the 1930's, Kurt Lewis developed a framework based on a leader's behavior. He argued that there are three types of leaders, namely: Autocratic, Democratic and Laissez-faire leaders. The best leaders are those who can use many different behavioral styles and choose the right style for each situation Based on this theory, it is clear that anybody can become a leader irrespective of one's gender because leaders are made.

2.5. Leadership and Management

(Robbins, 1992), Defines leadership as the ability to persuade others to willingly behave differently. The function of team leaders is to achieve the task set for them with the help of the grope. (Perry, E., Davis-Blake and Kulik, ., 1994), defines management as the guidance, Leadership and control of the efforts of a group of people toward some common objective. Thus, management is the process of setting and achieving organizational goals through its function while leadership is the ability to influence and guide to make others follows (Perry, E., Davis-Blake and Kulik., 1994),

(a) Planning: Planning focuses on the future: What is to be accomplished and how in essence, the planning function includes those managerial activities that determine objectives future and appropriate for the means for achieving those objectives.

(b) Organizing: According to (Robbins, 1992) organization is a comprehensive review in clear language about how to arrange matters so that people can work together effectively and well organizing is best illustrated by use of an organization chart, which highlight how work is divided and how it flows.

(c) Directing: Directing is the third function in the management cycle and one of the least understood partly because of the professional nature of much organization work and partly due to the destructive influence of political correctness, many department managers are reluctant to perform this function.

Controlling

Basically, organizational control is taking a systematic approach to figuring out if you're doing what you wanted to be doing or not. It's the part of planning after you've decided what you wanted to be doing. Management scholars agree that management is a distinct type of activity primarily responsible to get things done through other people.

2.6. Policy Overview at Global Level

The women empowerment has become an area of concern in development planning during the last few decades. The marginalization of women from development programs for a long period of time is challenged with changing policy perspectives from women in development (WID) which aims to include women in development projects. (DHS, 2005)

At international level, the Convention on Elimination of all forms of discrimination against women (CEDAW, 1979), the Beijing Platform For Action (BPFA, 1995) and Millennium Development Goals (MDG) are the main strategies and contentions introduced for the achievement of gender equality. CEDAW incorporates measures that governments have to take to guarantee gender equality: elimination of discrimination against women in employment opportunities and benefits of service; ensuring gender equality in all areas of socio-economic and political life. Ethiopia, as a member of the UN and signatory of the commitments has adapted the international conventions and agreements as domestic laws to promote gender equality in all spheres. As a means to implement these global agreements, different policies and legislations have been also enacted, such as the national policy of women, National population policy, education and training policy (1994), Cultural policy and other documents are formulated.

The historical legacy of inequality of discrimination suffered by women in Ethiopia is taken into account in order to remedy this legacy, are entitled affirmative measures. The purpose of such measures shall be for women's empowerment as to enable them to compete and participate on the basis of equality with men in political, social and economic life. Based on this practice at the grass root level must be compared with the above policies and other conventions.

2.7. The Women and Leadership in Ethiopia

Before the 1974 revolution, Ethiopian society has a strong religious base and the political culture has derived its strength from those religious beliefs. Orthodox Christianity was the dominant religion at the time forming the ideological base of the ruling monarchs. Within the stratification system, women were not only placed at the lowest hierarchical level, but were also expected to show utmost respect and submission to men and never question the motives of their husbands, fathers or male relatives. This hierarchy was also explicitly stated in the Fetha-Negest as cited (Biseswar, 2011)

Even though the first parliament was established in Ethiopia during Haile Selassie's regime, no woman had been given a chance of nomination. Latter, only 2 women in 1965 and 5 women in 1969 have occupied the imperial's parliament and the senate which had 250 and 125 seats respectively (Yalem, 2011).

The Federal Constitution of Ethiopia was promulgated in 1995 which has renewed the commitment to the gender policy and clearly expressed legislative support for women through its various articles. For example, Article 25 prohibits discrimination on grounds of gender. Article 35 is the most comprehensive law regarding women's rights and consists of nine sub-provisions. These are stipulations on the equal enjoyment of rights, equality of rights in marriage, entitlement to affirmative measures, freedom from harmful traditional practices, maternity leave, equal participation in program planning and implementation; equal rights on property ownership; equality in employment, and full access to reproductive health care. A number of other constitutional provisions, namely those embodied in Articles 7, 33, 38, 42, and 89, also have a direct bearing on the protection of the rights of Ethiopian women. Beside local efforts, the government in Ethiopia has always been among the first to become a signatory to many international conventions. It did not stop there, it was quite promising to see that the ruling party included them in an article constitution meant to domesticate these international treaties. Article 9 (4) in the 1995 constitution stipulates that "all international agreements ratified by Ethiopia are an integral part of the law of the land". Many other steps undertaken by the EFDRE government on women's rights include revision of the family law in 2000, revision of the penal code in 2004, revision of the labor law, launching of a social welfare policy in 1997, an educational policy, the formulation of a national health policy in 1993, the promulgation of a national population policy, an HIV/AIDS policy, and many more. Besides to these, Article 3 of the constitution provides equal opportunity for women to participate in the decision making process by giving them the right to vote and be elected. In this regard, a number of measures have been taken in terms of advocacy, lobbying and awareness creation in order to increase the participation of women in the decision making structures of the country.

Though much still remains to be done, there are noticeable achievements in the participation of women particularly in the parliament as well as in regional councils.

The Civil Service Reform Programs also contributed a lot to women's participation in decision making. Article 13 (1) of the Civil Service Proclamation No. 262/2002 prohibits discrimination among job seeker on the basis of sex. The proclamation also incorporates an affirmative action by stating that preference shall be given to female candidates who have equal or close scores to that of male candidates. As a result, the number of women indifferent decision making position has increased significantly.

2.8. Factors that Affect Women's Leadership and Decision Making Position

There are so many factors that hinder women from moving to decision making position and the major ones are described as follows.

2.8.1 Social/Cultural Factors

(Willis, 1991) Culture is that which surrounds us and plays a certain role in determining the way we behave at any given moment in time. By no means a static, concept defines culture and is both defined by events that are taking place both locally as well as regionally and internationally, it is shaped by individual events as well as collective ones, and it is a feature of the time or epoch we live in. Because it is so vast, culture is also often used as a tool to validate all manners of actions not, all of which may be acceptable to all concerned and are often intimately, connected to issues of identity. Cultural frameworks are not always imposed, but are open to manipulation and interpretation from many angles and sources.

According to Bernaars, as cited in (Mbugua, 2007) in any ethnic group in Africa a typical woman has low status particularly lack of power to make decisions on matters affecting her life and those of her family. This culturally determined expectation and attitude towards the girl child influences less allocation of resources towards the girl as compared to the boys. A boy will always be considered first before a girl. This gender biased cultural assumption and the subsequent differential treatment of boys and girls in a homestead not only diminish girls' access and performance in the education but also tend to push girls to doing the so called "feminine" careers. One of the earliest biological justifications for male superiority comes from Aristotle 5th century B.C as cited in (Amrot, 1998). He stated that the world is a hierarchy composed of ruling elements and women are "naturally" fit to the second. In his own words he described it as *"The male is naturally fitter to command than the female and female and women benefit most by being subject to male royal authority"*. It is mainly because during that time the inequality of men and women was a legally and socially accepted fact. Therefore, this simply shows his ideological difference from contemporary thinkers. While society believes in the superiority of men, we are in the decade of woman in which the involvement of women in many aspects is a hot issue.

A significant social feature resides in the double if not triple responsibilities of women. In most countries, women are perceived to have primary responsibilities as wives and mothers. But in many cases, either as a result of a preference for personal development, or out of sheer economic necessity, women also go out to work in the employment market. Managing these different occupations and their consequent responsibilities is no easy task for anyone man or woman (Willis, 1991).

2.8.2. Organizational Culture Barriers

According to Phillips as cited in (Mbugua, 2007) organizational culture is defined as the realities, values, symbols and rituals held in common by members of an organization and which contribute to the creation of norms and expectations of behavior. It defines conduct within an organization, determines what is and is not valued, and how authority is asserted.

The values, which support the great majority of organizations, and thus define success, often include money, power and status. As McKenna as cited in (Mbugua, 2007), the corresponding behaviors include working long hours and putting in face time (as proxies for productivity), competitiveness and a willingness to put work above all else. These values and behaviors, which some authors define as being masculine, have come to dominate organizations for historical and socio-economic reasons but are increasingly being challenged by women, and many men, who want to 'work to live' rather than 'live to work'.

The organizational and managerial values in some organizations tend to be characterized by stereotypical views of women's roles, attributes, preferences and commitments. These in turn influence decisions about who is suitable for particular positions, which is seen to have potential and so forth. When women find themselves selected or assessed on the basis of group membership rather than on their experience and abilities, they experience gender discrimination.

According to Eagly & Johannesen (as cited in Miller, 2006) leadership and management continue to be the domain of men that is 'thinks manager, think male'. This has implications for women and men, rightly or wrongly, are perceived in a particular way in society, which permeates organizations. They are assigned gender roles, which are shared beliefs that apply to individuals on the basis of their socially identified sex.

2.8.3. Gender Stereotype Factors

Gender stereotypes are generalized beliefs about the characteristics and qualities attributed to men and women in a society. In general, men are characterized as aggressive, risk-taking, decisive, and autonomous (agentic attributes), whereas women are characterized as kind, caring, relational, and humble (communal attributes) (Sikdar, Arijit & Mitra Sumit, 2008). Gender stereotypes can be described as the characteristics, attitudes, values and behaviors that society specifies as appropriate for the particular gender. The differences may have arisen not just from biological differences but also from sex role socialization during childhood and the way in which men and women develop psychologically. Gender stereotypes have consistently demonstrated that men are generally seen as more agent and more competent than women, while women are seen as more expressive and communal than men (Ginige, K. Amaratunga, D. & Haigh, R., 2007)

Gender stereotyping also explains why women and men are over-represented in particular types of jobs. Women dominate in "care" occupations such as nursing, teaching, social care and especially child-care. Men tend to be concentrated in construction and management areas associated with physical strength, risk-taking or decision-making. Such gender biases are also reflected in organizational practices. Male-dominated sectors tend to be more unionized, and men are more frequently selected for managerial positions because, some argue, they are perceived to be more willing to work longer hours and supervise others. Occupational, sectarian or time-related segregation can also be explained by women's preferences for job security or the manner in which societies force them to balance work and family responsibilities. These factors, among others including structural and legal context, could help explain the over-representation of women in public sector jobs and/or part-time work.

2.8.4. Work Place Policies

Women are not the same as men; they have particular biological functions that make them different, which in turn make their work experiences different. To this end, treating men and women the same has effectively created a systemic form of indirect discrimination for women. (Mbugua, 2007) asserts that pregnancy is a workplace issue that starts well before conception and ends long after birth. It is impossible to separate pregnancy and family responsibilities. Anecdotal evidence suggests assumptions that women will resign when they have children are still widespread and continue to form the basis for not hiring women among some employers. Large number of women report significant difficulties when they return to work due to the lack of supportive policies and practices in workplace. Issues like childcare, breastfeeding, flexible working hours and part-time work are still very current issues for most working women.

2.8.5. Discrimination in Appointments

Discrimination occur when an employee suffers unfavorable or unfair treatment due to their sex, race, religion, national origin, disabled or veteran status, or other legally protected characteristics. Federal law prohibits discrimination in a number of work-related areas, including recruiting, hiring, job evaluations, promotion policies, training, compensation and disciplinary action. Discrimination can be portrayed in different ways. It can occur in accessing employment, in promotion or in the treatment of an employee. According to UNDP report of 1999, despite the fact that many governments have adopted and adapted affirmative action measures and the rhetoric of gender balance, the figures still indicate that globally, despite the fact that women are half of the population, they are nowhere near half of the decision-making structures. The threshold of 30% advocated by the UNDP report, as a prelude to the 50% is still a dream for most women. As a matter of fact, intelligence, ability and motivation are the attributes of a good leader. These attributes are inherent in both men and women, and gender has no role to play in determining these attributes. However in pursuit to investigating the factors influencing women progression to leadership, social/cultural factors, organization culture, workplace policies and discrimination of women in appointments have come out clearly as the factors inhibiting women from moving up the ladder of upper managerial Positions.

2.8.6. Limited Access to Advanced Education

Education is a critical element to increase the upward socio-economic mobility of women and creates an opportunity to other hand, as educational background of women becomes less. The activities they perform tend to be less valued, and their low status is also perpetuated through the low value placed on their activity (Marshal et, al, 1999).

The fact that illiteracy rates are nearly always higher among women than men and it is a major limiting factor in women's contribution of development. The failure to eradicate and train female equally with male limits women's roles and makes them inadequately trained for employment opportunity that may be available (Wirth, 2005:25).

Therefore, having the right qualifications and training are central as policies and practices in the work place helps to eradicate discrimination at all levels (Ibid).

According to the United Nation Development Program (UNDP, 1995) report, out of the developing world's 900 million illiterate people, women outnumber men two to one, and girls constitute the majority of the 130 million children without access to primary school. Further, because population growth has superseded the expansion of women's education in some developing regions, the number of women who are illiterate has actually increased.

2.9. Related Empirical Literature

In global context, the number of women in leadership has risen, but only slowly. From 2004 to 2012, the percentage of women in leadership has risen five per cent at most. Between 2009 and 2011 the number fell from 24 per cent to 20 per cent, and in 2012 it stood at 21 per cent. In 2013, the number of women in leadership rose again to 24 per cent globally. (Women in senior managers: Still not enough 2012, 2; (Elsi, 2013)

The number of female senior managers in different countries changed a lot between 2012 and 2013. In 2012, Russia was leading with the most female senior managers but in 2013 the number fell from 46 per cent to 31 per cent. The high number of women in senior management in Russia was explained partly by the gender ratio and the rise of service sectors. China on the other hand increased its number of women in senior management notably. In 2012, 25 per cent of senior management were women; whereas in 2013 women constituted 51 per cent of senior managers and thus claimed theire place on the top of the list. Women's talents are more appreciated nowadays in China, especially in positions of higher-level. Countries like Japan and United Arab Emirates are highly patriarchal cultures and societies and thus the number of female managers is slow in those countries. (Elsi, 2013).

Gender equality in Administrative/leadership positions has not been easy to achieve. It requires hard work, long hours and are stressful. For women, this burden is added on to their child-care, home, and family responsibilities, a phenomenon referred to as the 'double shift' in Sader, et al. (2005).

One explanation given for the under representation of women in educational administration is that women themselves are the cause. It has been said that women are sometimes reluctant to run for public office, are not assertive, do not want power, or are unwilling to play the game (Growe, R. & Montgomery, P., 2000). Women also tend to see other women as threats, leaving successful women unsupported in confronting discrimination (sexism, racism), and the 'old boys' network' (de la Rey, 2005, Sader, et al. 2005). For women to develop the confidence to take up leadership there is need for support from other women.

Empirical studies in the USA carried out by Inglehart and Norris (2003) show that,

> When women are economically disadvantaged, it is much more difficult for them to break into electoral office because they do not have access to necessary resources in the realm of public decision making.

Empirical studies done by (Shvedova2007) suggests that in most countries women are carrying a disproportionate share of domestic work .It must be recognized that it is difficult for women to participate in political life when their major concern is survival and they have no choice but to spend much of their time trying to fulfill the basic needs of families. In addition to that, however, some women may have full time jobs as wives and mothers as well as other full careers. Becoming a member of parliament in these conditions might then be considered a third full-time job. The result is that most women think that they cannot hold a political office along with other responsibilities. (Oduol 2008)

Empirical studies in Nigeria shows that the society is permeated by patriarchy whereby women are expected to conform and confine themselves to male dominance and female subservience. Women are seen to belong to the home, be capable of making sound decisions and it is unbecoming of women to expose themselves in public for political activities such as campaign rallies .Men often find it incredible and impracticable to see women participating in politics (Iloh and Ikena 2009).

2.10 Research Gap of the Study

Many studies have been conducted regarding women's participation in decision making positions. Among the studies, Brkti G. (2014), An Assessment of factors Affecting Participation of women in Management Positions, The Case of Ethio-Telecom Company and Kinfe Tekle (2016), Assessing Contributing Factors for Under Representation of Women in Management, The Case of Addis Ketema Sub City Administration are cited in this research.

These studies did not assess the current status of women's participation in decision making positions, the existing policy framework and men's perception towards women's participation in decision making positions.

Besides to the abovementioned studies, Saron Wakjira (2016), Factors Affecting Women's Participation in Decision Making Positions, The Case of ADHA Administration was also cited. Though this study has included the gaps identified above, it was made out of Addis Ababa.

To address the gaps identified above, this research has assess and describe the current status of women's participation in decision making positions, men's perception towards women's participation in decision making positions, and has examined the existing policy framework towards women's participation in decision making positions.

2.11. Conceptual Framework

Reichel and Ramey (1987) in Kombo and Tromp, (2006) have seen conceptual framework as a set of ideas and principles taken from relevant field of inquiry and used to structure subsequent presentations. Conceptual framework involves forming ideas about relationships between variables in the study and showing these relationships graphically or diagrammatically (Mugenda and Mugenda, 2003).

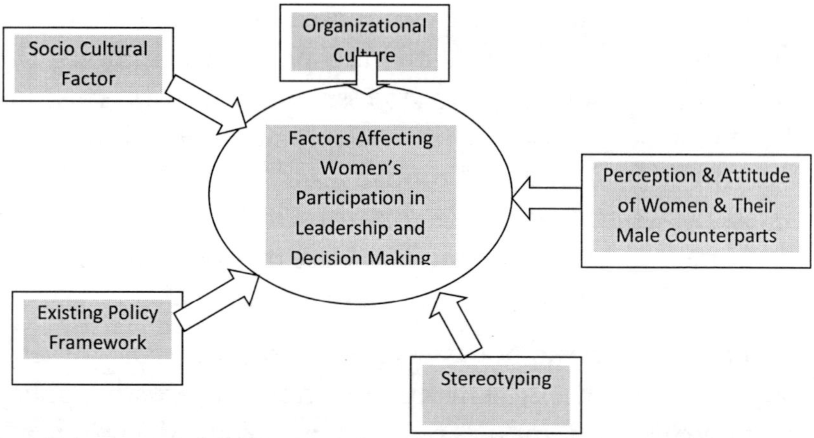

Source: Developed from the Literature Review.

Figure 2.1. Conceptual Framework on Factors Affecting Women Participation in Leadership.

The above model explains that the relationship between the dependent and independent variables used in the study. The dependent variable is women's participation in leadership where as the major independent variables are composed of socio cultural factor, organizational culture, existing policy framework, stereotyping and perception & attitude of women & their male counterparts towards women leaders. The collection of these independent variables negatively affects women's participation in leadership.

Chapter Three

Research Methodology

3.1. Definition of Research Methodology

Research methodology is the specific procedures or techniques used to identify, select, process, and analyze information about a topic. In a research paper, the methodology section allows the reader to critically evaluate a study's overall validity and reliability. The methodology section answers two main questions: How was the data collected or generated? How was it analyzed?

3.2. Research Methods

The research has used descriptive type of research design because it helps to describe the factors that affect women's participation in leadership and decision making position. Descriptive research studies are concerned with describing characteristics of a particular, individual, or of group (Kothari, 2004)

Identifying the determinants that affect women's participation in leadership and decision making requires mix of both quantitative and qualitative research methods for the study. According to (Collical, 2009), quantitative methods are information about a phenomenon in numerical form either counts or measurement while qualitative information gathered that is not in numerical form and encourage free and natural response from participants, often in the form of unrestricted talk. Field surveying technique was employed to generate quantitative data while focus group discussion and key informant interview with unstructured and semi structured open ended questionnaires was used for qualitative data generation. This helped the study to generate pertinent data and have better insight as women's participation influenced by different factors.

3.3. Sampling Frame

The sample frame for the study was the leaders and employee existing in Bole Sub City Administration, (Eight Public Sectors and 3 Woredas). The list of the public sectors, employees and leaders are the sampling frame of the study.

Table 3.1. Sample Frame

S/N	*Respondent Particulars*	*Total Population*		
		Male	*Female*	*Total*
1.	Women, Child and Youth	19	17	36
2.	Public Service	47	67	114
3.	Finance and Economic Development	20	30	50
4.	Trade office			
5.	Education	28	31	59
6.	Human resource and Social Affairs	11	6	17
7.	Industry development office			
8.	Council Office			
9.	Woreda 1	18	7	25
10.	Woreda 6	19	7	26
11.	Woreda 12	21	8	29
	Total	**183**	**173**	**356**

3.4. Population and Sampling

3.4.1. Population

The target population of this study will be 356 and grouped in to positions such as

- Top level leaders of the selected sectors and selected 3 Woredas
- Core process owners of the selected sectors
- Middle level (supportive process owners) of selected sectors
- Employees of selected sectors of the sub city.

The researcher has chosen this population because they can deliver appropriate information about the subject that is under investigates in this research. Since they are working in public organization they have got a chance to know hindering factors that affect women's participation in leadership and decision making position.

3.4.2. Sample size and Sampling Techniques

To attain feasibility principle of research, the researcher has taken sample or respondents from target population through different sampling techniques based on the nature of data or information required. Among 20 public sectors of the sub city, eight (8) Sectors (Women, Child and Youth, Public Service, Finance and Economic Development, Education, Industry Development office, Human Resource and Social Affairs, Trade office, and the Council office of the Sub City are selected. These sectors were taken purposively since the sectors are assumed to be vast and responsible bodies for issues related to leadership and decision making area.

Besides to these sectors, three Woreda leaders out of fourteen are taken based on probability sampling technique.

Furthermore, the researcher has selected the direct respondents for the study through both probability and non- probability method. Briefly speaking, the office leaders of the selected sample sectors are selected purposively for interview questions with the objective to give more explanation on key issues since they are considered as the one who shoulder greater responsibility on women's and related issues. On the other hand, other employees of the sample sectors are selected through simple random probability technique to allow them get equal opportunity to fill the self-administered questionnaires.

3.4.3. Sample Size Determination

To determine the total sample size to be used for the study, the researcher has used the statistical formula for known size of population. After that, the researcher has used different sampling techniques to breakdown the total sample to different individual employee of the sectors for better use of the samples.

According to (Israel, 2009), if the number of total population is known, $n=N/1+N(e^2)$ formula is used to determine total samples. This will be used for the study and precision level estimated.

Where, n = sample size

N = population from which sample will be taken

e = error that will be tolerated

In addition, (Jackson, 2003), the relationship between sample size and precision/confidence level is simple. To increase the level of confidence, sample size must be increased sufficiently and 95% is the usual level of confidence used in a research tolerating 5% of error estimation. Accordingly, the target population of the study is 356 and the estimated level of tolerated error is 5% to increase confidence level of the study, thus, applying the above formula the size of the sample became 188 employees. This is computed as follows,

$$n=N/1+N(e^2),\ n=356/1+(356x.05^2),\ 356/1.89\ =\ 188$$

3.4. 4. Data Source

For the fulfillment of this study, the researcher substantially has relied on the primary sources of data. The main sources of the data were the sample civil servants that were contacted through field survey, interview, and focus group discussion. To obtain the required information, structured and unstructured interviews were conducted. For the opinion of the relevant bodies, self administered questionnaire (both closed and open ended questions) were distributed to the samples. On the other hand the researcher had organized two focus group discussions to get matured and common understanding of the respondents that helped the researcher to have detail understanding of the issues that were asked through other techniques. Furthermore, the researcher has included secondary data source to have detail understanding of concepts, variables of measurement and other's view point out the topic. These include different books, articles, dissertations, internet, reports and plan.

3.4.5. Data Collection Methods and Instruments

The data collection techniques that were used to collect first hand information were self administered questionnaires, depth interviews and focus group discussions.

A. Questionnaires (Closed-Ended and Open-Ended)

The questionnaires were administered according to the sample size e determined for employees except leaders of each sector to be sampled. Accordingly 167 employees were required to fill self administered questionnaires. This is because that questionnaires especially close ended ones can help the researcher to easily quantify and increase the objectivity of the result while open ended questionnaires can help to capture broader idea and qualitative data from respondents. Out of the 167 employees' to whom the questionnaires distributed, 164 respondents (86 female and 78 male) have responded.

The questionnaires were developed in English. These were distributed using simple random sampling technique of probability sampling method for the expert employee's and purposive sampling to all process owners of the offices to be sampled. These process owners were assumed to be as one of the decision making positions.

B. Interview (Structured and Unstructured)

As it was believed that it helps to collect clear and deep information, the researcher has used interview techniques. Purposive technique was used in interviewing five individuals of the head /vice head of the offices. These groups of respondents were expected to have matured and well organized idea on the questions and issues they were asked. When interviewing the respondents, the researcher has used list of questions and other oral questions on some critical issues that cannot be reached otherwise.

C. Focus Group Discussion

In addition to the aforementioned techniques, the researcher has used focus group discussion that helped her to investigate a more detailed explanation and ideas that reflect the common understanding of the leaders of Woredas on the objectives of the study. This was done through coordination of three group discussion each group having eight members, which was designed to include equal proportions of both male and female participants.

3.4.6. Methods of Data Analysis and Presentation

For the purpose of achieving the objectives of the study, data that were gathered through these different techniques were analyzed and interpreted qualitatively and quantitatively. To this effect, data that were gathered through questionnaires were analyzed quantitatively and displayed in central tendency measures in the tables. To this effect, mean score and standard deviation are used to describe the result for objectives other than the attitudes and awareness level of women and their men counter parts that were analyzed and interpreted. In parallel, the descriptive measures were used to describe the same issue the way it displays to what extent the view vary between women and their counterpart men. On the other hand, the information acquired from respondents profile are displayed by using numeric representation, percentages after which it was presented in tabular format.

Similarly, data that are gathered through interviews and focus group discussions are analyzed qualitatively based on classification of their respective thematic area and issues along with the specific objectives and variables used to measure the concepts included in the study. In most cases, these qualitative data are interpreted in line with the data that were gathered by questionnaires especially in the discussion part of the study.

Statistical package for the social sciences (SPSS) version 22 and Microsoft office Excel Windows 2007 were used to analyze the data gathered by closed ended questionnaires as they assisted the researcher to manage the data objectively.

3.4.7. Ethical Consideration of the Study

While conducting the study, the researcher has considered research's ethical principles. Primarily, the researcher has ensured that there would no exploitation for personal gain of research population. Secondly, the researcher did not use influence over respondents, or other to enforce them to participate in the research. In addition, the researcher has taken in to account; the culture, religion, gender, and other significant differences within the researcher population .The researcher has used the data for the intended purpose that is for the academic purpose only.

Chapter Four

Data Presentation, Analysis and Interpretation

4.1. Demographic Data

In order to have the comprehensive information on important variables that may allow a researcher to analyze variables required to include in the objective of the study, it is important to include the demographic data of respondents. This is because the researcher could infer some hints regarding the issue related to the study. Table 4.1 below shows the demographic data of respondents that were used in the study.

Table 4.1. Demographic Data of Respondents (n = 164)

Variable	*Category*	*Frequency*	*Percent*
Sex	Female	86	52.4
	Male	78	47.6
Age in Years	Below 20		
	21-30	93	56.7
	31-40	57	34.8
	41-50	11	6.7
	Above 50	3	1.8
Work Experience in Years	1-2	8	4.9
	3-7	85	51.8
	8-13	52	31.7
	14-20	14	8.5
	Above 20	5	3.0

(Contd...)

Educational Status	Certificate	8	4.9
	Diploma	2	1.2
	Bachelor Degree	148	90.2
	Second degree	6	3.7
	PhD and Above		
Marital Status	Married	117	71.3
	Unmarried	40	24.4
	Divorced	7	4.3
Current Position	Office Head		
	Process Owner	45	27.4
	Expert	113	68.9
	Supportive Workers	6	3.7
Total			

Source: Own Field Survey, 2019.

The above table 4.1 shows that 52.4 percent of respondents were female while 47.6 percent were male. Therefore, though female respondents were greater in number of the distribution, both sexes were well represented that indicates the samples were the representative of the population. As can be seen from table 4.1, the respondents' age groups fall in four age categories designed by the researcher. The highest number of the respondents (56.7%) falls in the age group of 21-30 and 34.8% of respondents fall in the age group of 31-40. The rest 8.5% fall in the age group above 40. This result shows almost all respondents were old enough to participate in the process of providing data information for the study. Though different age groups were included in the study, the result shows that the majority of the respondents (91.5%) were youngsters (in the age group of 21-40).

The above table 4.1 also portrays that the respondents have different years of work experience that can lay a ground to understand to what extent the respondents have exposure regarding social, economical, cultural and political work place condition and related issues. Accordingly, the least experienced respondents (1-2 years) holds 4.9% where as the highest number of respondents 51.8% falls in the interval from 3 to 7 years of experience followed by 31.7% in the interval of 8 to 13 years. The rest (11.5%) have 14 years of work experience.

The same table also shows the participants of the study have different educational background. Accordingly, the highest numbers of the respondents (90.2%) were bachelor degree holders while 3.7% of the respondents are second degree holders. The rest, 4.9% and 1.2% of the respondents were certificate and diploma holders respectively and none of the respondents are PhD holders.

From the analysis, one can conclude that the respondents have enough years of work experience that enable them to explain and describe issues related to the status of women in leadership and decision making positions and challenges that undermine women's participation in leadership and decision making position. It is also possible to infer from the result of the analysis that the majority of the respondents' educational status had enabled them to give matured response regarding the case understudy.

Regarding marital status of the, the majority of respondents table 4.1 above shows that (71.3%) were married while the least number of the respondents (4.3%) were divorced and the rest 24.4% were unmarried. Thus, from this, it is possible to deduce that the majority of the respondents were well familiar with the issue of gender and opposite sex relation in terms of social, economical, cultural and issues that directly or indirectly affect the women's potential in any development program.

As one can see in the above table, 68.9% of the respondents are experts while 27.4% are process owners and the rest 3.7% supportive workers who mainly perform the ordinary activities like cleaners etc. From the above table, it is possible to conclude that the majority of the respondents were experts. Therefore, the uneven distribution of position among male and female plays greater role in understanding factors affecting women's participation in leadership and decision making position.

4.2. The Current Status of Women's Participation in Leadership and Decision Making Position

For the determination of current status of women's participation in leadership and decision making position, the researcher organized the collected data in such a way that enables one to explain it in terms of the job position or the title of the position in the organization they were serving and sex wise. Thus, the current status of women's participation in leadership and decision making position in terms of their positioning the organization and sex ground that may help see the reflection of gaps in their appointments for the sampled sectors is shown in table 4.2 below.

Table 4.2. The Eight Public Institutions Target Employees Position by Sex (N=282)

No	*Title*	*Male*		*Female*		*Total*		*Remark*
1.	Office Head		%		%		%	These were purposely selected for data gathering through interview
		6	75	2	25	8	100	
2.	Process Owner	27	71	11	29	38	100	
3.	Expert	108	47	121	53	229	100	
4.	Others such as Cleaners			15	100	15	100	
	Total	141		149		290		

Source: Documents (Employees list) from Selected Sectors of Bole Sub-City.

Table 4.2 above shows that 2 female & 6 male leaders were assigned as office head. On the same manner, 27 male and 11 female were assigned as process owners. On the other hand, there were 108 male experts while there were 121 female experts and 15 female supportive employees like cleaners. From the above analysis regarding the current status of women's participation in leadership and decision making position, one can understand that majority of the decision making positions (75% of office heads and 71% of the process owner) are occupied by male while only 25% and 29% of the office heads and process owners respectively are occupied by female. On the other hand majority (53% of experts and 100% of the supportive employees) of the non-decision making positions are occupied by female employees.

Generally, according to the professional understanding of the researcher, it is possible to infer that though there was a sort of participation of female employees in the leadership and decision making position, it requires strict attention from management and concerned bodies especially to bring improvement in the areas of position that are considered as inferior position and non-decision making positions.

The researcher, to have a detail understanding and to provide comprehensive explanations, had collected data on how the leaders are assigned to the leadership and decision making positions.

Table 4.3. How did the Majority of Leaders and Decision Makers get these Positions

S/No	*Options*	*Frequency*	*Percent*
1.	Through work performance in the form of promotion	37	22.6
2.	Through recommendation of boss	53	32.3
3.	Through long service years in the organization	14	8.5
4.	Through merit based	9	5.5
5.	Through Network and relationship	51	31.1
	Total	164	100.0

Source: Own field Survey 2019.

As one can see from table 4.3 above, (32.3%) of respondents responded that leaders and decision makers came to their position through recommendation of boss and 31.1% of the respondents responded that leaders came to their position through network and relationship while 22.6% of them replied that leaders came to their position through work performance in the form of promotion. The rest of the respondents that is 8.5% and 5.5% have responded that leaders came to their position through long service years in the organization and through merit based respectively.

From the above table one can understand that result of the respondents has the reflection that majority of the leaders and decision makers were given their position through recommendation of boss and through network & relationships. The issue here is that to what extent these methods of assigning leaders free from bias are. In other words, this kind of narrow grounds to appoint a leader or a decision maker to the position may not be efficient and participatory in nature that these sorts of practices possibly affect especially potential females to come to leadership and decision making position.

The above table also shows that the least number of respondents replied that the leaders and decision makers got their position through merit based manner (through competition). Looking this response in professional eyes, one can recognize that there was great problem in the way the practitioners appoint the leaders and decision makers that affect and discourage the habit of developing basic grounds for completion. It is also possible to infer from the analysis that though there was a seemingly better in appointing leaders and decision makers through work performance in the form of promotion, still there was problem in using experienced employees that could be inferred from the response rate sited above indicating that women were appointed with consideration of their service year.

Therefore, it can be concluded from the response of the respondents that most of leaders and decision makers come to position through relations, networks and other informal means which indicates that there are no clear and established rules regarding selecting leaders and decision makers. This approach may directly or indirectly affect women's empowerment.

4.3. Attitudes and Awareness of Women and Their Men Counterparts about Women's Competency in Leadership and Decision Making Position.

The researcher had tried to test the attitude and awareness of women and men regarding women's competency in leadership and decision making position using various dimensions. These dimensions were Assertiveness, Confidence, Perception and Awareness. These dimensions are also tested using different points and are presented in the following tables (Table 4.4. – 4.7) followed by respective analysis.

Table 4.4. Assertiveness (n = 164)

No	*Item*	*Sex*	*Descriptive Statistics*	
			Mean	*SD*
1.	Surely, women can be competent in managing every activity of public institution like men.	Female	3.13	1.12
		Male	3.17	1.08
2.	It is convincing to say that women are not capable of solving problems the same as men	Female	2.57	1.21
		Male	2.53	1.19
3.	Women have sound mind as men have	Female	3.34	1.17
		Male	3.31	1.12
4.	Women usually make efficient and effective decision as men.	Female	2.50	1.20
		Male	2.33	1.14

Source: Own field Survey 2019.

As it is seen in the above table, there is no significant difference with respect to item No. 1 ("women can be competent in managing every activity of public institution like men"). Though the difference between gender is not significant, the item is rated as average both by male (M=3.17, SD=1.08) and female (M=3.13, SD=1.12) respondents. In the same manner, there is no significant difference regarding item No 2 & 3 ("women are not capable of solving problems the same as men" and "Women have sound mind as men have"). There is only minor difference between the response of female and male showing that female (mean = 2.5, SD = 1.80) and male (mean = 2.33, SD = 1.14) in the fourth item ("Women usually make efficient and effective decision as men").

From the above analysis, one can understand that the response for both male and female on the variables used to measure the concept of assertiveness dimension is statistically insignificant difference. In other way, though there is a relative difference in the case of some items in terms of the mean and standard deviation it is not possible to say there is great difference between the response of male and female except it shows some minor reflection of difference the concept of assertiveness that is in their ability to stand for their right that is the concept of assertiveness.

The Focus Group Discussion (FGD) response shows that there is significant difference between male and female in assertiveness that is the concept used to reflect to what extent female are standing for their right in a convincing manner in respect to their male counter parts. This could be understood especially from the group's explanation of men are always / averagely more assertive than women and women are less assertive than men that directly affects their participation in the position of leadership and decision making .The other important idea raised by the FGD was that the female themselves discourage themselves that they are less assertive regarding standing for one's own right and benefit.

Furthermore, the interview response reveals that there is significant difference between male and female respondents regarding the issues assertiveness that could be understand from their reflection of their ideas in such a way that male are usually convincing in their assertion and their judgment in every public and private issues whether it is economic or social issues.

Thus, the general analysis of the study on the concept allows us to understood that there was a seemingly deference between the objective response and the open discussion and interviews. This can evoke us to take decisions like there is problem regarding assertiveness dimension that underestimate females.

Table 4.5. Confidence (n=164)

No	*Item*	*Sex*	*Descriptive Statistics*	
			Mean	*SD*
1.	Men are more confident than women in decision making	Female	2.12	1.06
		Male	2.15	1.19
2.	Women can reason out their point of view	Female	1.41	.49
		Male	1.44	.59
3.	Women and men can equally hesitate to accept others' views or decisions	Female	2.66	1.26
		Male	2.51	1.23
4.	Men are usually with a better mood than women in leadership and decision	Female	3.07	1.11
		Male	3.22	1.06

Source: Own field Survey 2019.

The above table shows that there is no significant statistical difference between male and female respondents i.e male (Mean= 2.15, SD=1.19) and female (Mean= 2.12, SD=1.06) with respect to the item "Men are more confident than women in decision making". In the same table one can see that there is no significant statistical difference between the respondents i.e female (Mean= 1.41, SD=0.49 and male

(Mean= 1.44, SD=0.59) with respect to the item "Women can reason out their point of view". Regarding items 3 (Women and men can equally hesitate to accept others' views or decisions) Mean and Standard Deviation of the respondents is female (Mean=2.66, SD=1.26) and male (Mean=2.51, SD=1.23). In the same manner the mean and standard deviation for female and male for item 4 (Men are usually with a better mood than women in leadership and decision), is female (Mean=3.07 SD=1.11) and male (Mean= 3.22, SD=1.06). In both cases (items 3 & 4) there is slight difference in the Mean and Standard Deviation of the Female and Male respondents' response. From the above analysis one can understand that the response for both male and female on the variables used to measure the concept of "confidence" dimension is statistically insignificant difference. In other way, though there is a relative difference in the case of some items in terms of the mean, it is not possible to say there is great difference between the response of male and female except it shows some minor reflection of difference in their ability to be confident and independent in their action and decision making that is the concept of confidence. From the same analysis, it is possible to deduce that females are arguing that they are confident in their decision making and leading their responsibility while their counter parts men are more pessimistic about women's confidence.

The Focus group discussion (FGD) response shows that there is significant difference between male and female in confidence dimension that is the concept used to reflect to what extent female are confident in their action, decision making and leadership activities relative to their male counter parts. This could be understood especially from the groups' explanation of "women are usually less confident than their male counter parts" that directly affects their participation in the position of leadership and decision making in many aspects. The other important idea raised by the FGD, regarding this issue, was that the females discourage themselves that they are less confident in accomplishing their responsibility to the standard they are expected.

Furthermore, the interview response reveals that there is significant difference between male and female respondents regarding the confidence issues. According to the interview response from the majority of the respondents, "women are less confident than men in their decision making position and their counter parts men are more confident in all aspects". The interview respondents said that the female underestimate themselves that directly impact their lives even beyond their participation in leadership and decision making position.

Thus, the general analysis of the study on the confidence concept allows us to understand that the male parts of the respondents persist that women are less confident than their counter parts men. The other major idea they raised regarding this issue is that in judging their own issue women seek males support and also they reflected that men can decide on women's and men's issues and agendas in independent manner.

Table 4.6. Perception (n=164)

No	*Item*	*Sex*	*Descriptive Statistics*	
			Mean	*SD*
1.	In my opinion, women can occupy and manage any responsibility and issues even in certain cases, more than men certainly	Female	2.27	1.07
		Male	2.18	1.07
2.	It is true that men's contribution is more vital in development than women	Female	2.26	1.07
		Male	2.35	1.06
3.	Women's activity involves creativity and innovativeness as men	Female	2.21	1.10
		Male	2.19	1.08
4.	Men and women can equally shoulder equal weight of responsibility	Female	1.63	.72
		Male	1.62	.70

Source: Own field Survey 2019.

Table 4.6 above shows that there is only slight statistical difference between the response of female and male with respect to all the items stated in the table. This is revealed by the mean and standard deviation of each sex for each item. Regarding item No 1 that says "women can occupy and manage any responsibility and issues even in certain cases, more than men certainly", mean for female and male is 2.27 and 2.18 respectively while standard deviation is 1.07 for both female and male respondents. For item No 2 that says "It is true that men's contribution is more vital in development than women", mean for female and male is 2.26 and 2.35 respectively while standard deviation is 1.07 and 1.06 for female and male respectively. In the same manner, the mean and standard deviation for item No 3 that says "Women's activity involves creativity and innovativeness as men" mean for female and male is 2.21 and 2.19 respectively while standard deviation is 1.10 and 1.08 for female and male respectively. Regarding the last item that says "Men and women can equally shoulder equal weight of responsibility", mean for female and male is 1.63 and 1.62 respectively while standard deviation is 0.72 and 0.70 for female and male respectively.

From the above analysis, one can understand that the response from both male and female on the variables used to measure the concept of "perception" dimension is almost the same except slight difference. Though the mean of normal distribution of all the variables are below average (below 2.5), it is possible to deduce that, regardless of the underestimating perception of their male counterparts, female have the perception that they are capable of occupying leadership and decision making positions. This shows us that women are more optimistic about themselves than the attitude men hold about the female's potential of occupying the positions that has negative connotations. Also it is possible to deduce from the study that in almost all the variables of measurement of the "perception" men's perception/attitude discourages women from participating in leadership and decision making position and beyond this it affects women's actual role in deciding their personal and social issues and benefits.

In addition, the interview response reveals that there is significant difference between male and female respondents regarding the perception dimension. According to the interview response from ths majority of respondents, "women are optimistic than men in occupying leadership and decision making position and their counter parts men are more pessimistic almost in all aspects. The interview respondents said that though both males and females are not fully recognizing, males underestimate women's role that directly impact women's lives even beyond their participation in leadership and decision making position.

Furthermore, FGD response shows that there is significant difference between male and female in perception dimension that is the concept used to reflect to what extent female are holding positive attitudes towards themselves in their action, decision making and leadership activities relative to their male counter parts. According to the reflections of the focus groups' ideas, men hold attitudes with negative connotations towards their counter parts women. The average response from the FGD has the tendency to hold the idea that men are pessimistic about women's capability while relatively women are more optimistic about themselves regarding their ability and potential to occupy the leadership and decision making positions.

Thus the general understanding of analysis of the study on the perception dimension lets us to understand that the male respondents persist that women are less capable than their men counter parts. In other words, the female group holds a more optimistic and a more flexible attitude/ perceptions about their ability to make decision and lead the public and their resource as men do.

Table 4.7. Awareness (n = 164)

No	*Item*	*Sex*	*Descriptive Statistics*	
			Mean	*SD*
1.	Almost all the time, your colleagues give attachment to issue of empowering women	Female	2.44	1.09
		Male	2.44	1.11
2.	The employees of your office are flexible enough in solving gender related problems	Female	2.88	1.27
		Male	2.74	1.29
3.	The management of your office encourages employees to put effort with intention to increase women' participation in leadership and decision making	Female	2.17	1.02
		Male	2.12	1.00
4.	Now, I know that women are as competent as men	Female	3.60	1.10
		Male	3.59	1.06
5.	I can now recognize that women can organize and manage competitively as their men counterparts	Female	3.21	1.13
		Male	3.18	1.15

Source: Own field Survey 2019.

As it is seen in Table 4.7 above, the response of female and male to item No 1 that says "Almost all the time, your colleagues give attachment to issue of empowering women" is mean 2.44 for both and standard deviation is 1.09 for female and 1.11 for male which shows slight statistical difference. When we see the second item "The employees of your office are flexible enough in solving gender related problems", the response is female (Mean = 2.88, SD = 1.27) and male (Mean = 2.74, SD =1.29) with slight statistical difference. The response for item No 3 "The management of your office encourages employees to put effort with intention to increase women' participation in leadership and decision making "is female (Mean = 2.17, SD = 1.02) and male (Mean = 2.12, SD = 1.00) with slight statistical difference. It is also shown on the same table that the response for the fourth item "women are as competent as men" is female (Mean = 3.60, SD = 1.10) and male (mean = 3.59, SD = 1.06) which also shows a slight statistical difference. Lastly, the response of the respondent for the fifth item "women are as competent as men" is female (Mean = 3.21, SD = 1.13) and male (mean = 3.18, SD = 1.15) which the difference is the same as the other items in the table.

From the above analysis one can understand that the response from both male and female on the variables used to measure the awareness level of the respondents is almost similar with slight statistical difference.

The analysis shows that the response of both men and women do not have significant difference in their level of awareness on the issues reflecting the level of participation of women in leadership and decision making positions.

In addition to the above analysis, the interview response reveals that there is statistically slight difference between male and female respondents regarding recognizing the importance and readiness of women in decision making and leadership positions. According to the interview response from the majority of the respondents women are more aware of their importance in decision making and leadership position than their male counterparts almost in all aspects.

FGD response shows that there is significant difference between male and female in awareness dimension that is the concept used to reflect to what extent female are proactive enough and to what extent they are alerted and open to change towards themselves in their action, decision making and leadership activities relative to their male counterparts. According to the reflections of focus groups' idea, women are more likely to recognize the importance and openness of women to change than their male counterparts. The average response from the FGD has the tendency to hold the idea that men are with less awareness and more pessimistic about the importance of women's capability in making decision and being in leadership position.

If we combine the analysis from the different methods, one can understand that women and their counterparts men are not educed with internalized awareness that can influence them to recognize the importance of women's participation in leadership and decision making positions. In other words, the analysis gives the insight that enables one to decide in such a way that though there are different programs for awareness raising, there are still problems in implementing the awareness raising programs that can be understood from the reluctances of getting out of old attitudes that persists in defending women not to fully participate in leadership and decision making positions.

4.4. How well the Existing Policy Framework is Designed to Encourage Women's Participation in Leadership and Decision Making Position.

It is possible to say effective and efficient policy framework lays ground for successful implementation of program, plan, projects and different activities that are intended in a social, economical, cultural and political sphere of a certain country or a sector like our public and business sectors. So, this research had a policy framework issues as one of its area of attention. The following table 4.8 summarizes and describes the respondents' response rate that further tells us how well the existing policy framework was designed to encourage women's participation in leadership and decision making position.

Table 4.8. How well the Existing Policy Framework is Designed to Encourage Women's Participation in Leadership and Decision Making Position.

No.	*Statements of Question*	*Mean*	*SD*
1.	The existing policy framework is supportive and can build women's capacity that make them compete for leadership and in decision making positions without compromising quality	2.96	1.24
2.	The existing policy framework of the institution/office are problem solving in nature especially in issues related to gender and women's empowerment.	2.93	1.25
3.	The different principles and guidelines at the office are context specific and applicable in the real situation of the offices capacity to bring women to leadership and decision making positions in a competitive and healthy way.	2.47	1.48
4.	The existing gender and women's empowerment policy frame work has been developed with clear and specific indicators that allow to conduct effective and efficient monitoring and evaluation	2.85	1.33
5.	The different principles and guidelines on policy frameworks of your office allow and support self learning and cooperation that enable women to deal with issues either individually or in team and/or in both	2.97	1.24
6.	The different principles and guidelines or policy frameworks of the office are comprehensive and sound	2.49	1.48

Source: Own Field Survey, 2019.

According to the above table the respondent's response on the dimension of supportive measure of the concept the average (mean) response rate was 2.96 and the distribution of scores around the mean was the standard deviation of 1.24 that shows the average response rate of the respondents was very close to each other. Likewise, the average response rate for the policy framework problem solving nature was 2.93 and standard deviation of 1.25 that shows consistence of response distribution around the mean score. In addition, the above table shows us that the mean score for context specificity of the policy was 2.47 and standard deviation of 1.48 while the mean score for whether the policy framework is endowed with clear indicators aiding in efficient and effective monitoring and evaluation was 2.85 having standard deviation of 1.33. Furthermore, the same table shows that the extent of the policy framework regarding its nature to allow self learning and cooperation earned the average response of 2.97 which is relatively better than the other measurement dimensions used to determine the concept or the objective. The frequent response for learning and cooperation dimension was too similar to other variables with standard deviation of 1.21 while the comprehensiveness and soundness earned the average of 2.49 and got standard deviation 1.48 that shows relatively the most dispersed response distribution around the mean score.

The above table comprehensively shows us that the standard deviation (average distribution) of scores around the mean value of normal distribution was around 1 unit that has the reflection of concentration of responses. This further shows us that the respondents were having similar opinion on the issue.

The professional understanding of the researcher can forward that the average response rate for all the variables used to measure the nature of the existing policy framework in different dimensions earned the average value of less than the highest possible mean value. Furthermore, all the variables employed to measure the objectives did not earn the value on the scale greater than the possible average that reveals the respondent's view of the policy framework inefficiency and that there is problem with policy framework. In othe words, the respondent's response was so consistent and concentrated in their distribution around the average score that provide further understanding of similarity of respondents' view towards the nature of the existing policy framework.

In addition to the above analysis, the data gathered through interview reveals that the problem arises from the implementation problems that is mostly reflected from the interviewees' persistence in diverting the issues to the poor implementation and that the great problem tends to be how the implementation process is carried out.

Furthermore, the response from the FGD asserts that though there are some problems with the nature of the policy, the fact still exists in the implementation stage of the policy. The majority of the group members forwarded that the policy is somewhat good but they tried to locate the problem to the administration and those who are expected to implement the policy.

From the whole analysis of the concept that the result acquired through questionnaire and other two methods, the FGD and interview, seems opposing each other. But, internally, it is not opposing each other rather the average and comprehensive understanding of the result reveals that the poor implementation of the policy made the respondents to push complaints on he policy itself.

4.5. Factors Affecting Women's Participation in Leadership and Decision Making Position

To have a detail understanding of all the concept that were

considered in the study, the researcher tried to dig out the major factors affecting women's participation in leadership and decision making positions. To this effect, the researcher asked respondents by preparing relevant questions that enable to understand opinions and rate the view in a more understandable way.

Table 4.9. Factors Affecting Women's Participation in Leadership and Decision Making Position

Variable	*Statement/Question*	*Mean*	*SD*
Social /cultural Factors	The attitude of our community is discouraging women to participate in leadership and decision making positions	2.84	1.10
	Basically, it is possible to say our culture is a major barrier for women's participation in leadership and decision making positions	3.04	1.30
	The majority of our community believe to the participation and capacity of women in the involvement in the different development programs	2.09	1.22
Organizational Culture	Our organization does not have the habit of exerting available resources and capacities to increase women's participation in leadership and decision making positions	2.81	1.43
	Usually the employees of your office do not appreciate your organization for its pro-activeness in encouraging women to leadership and decision making positions	2.79	1.30
	You can judge that the structural arrangement of your office is not applicable and conducive enough to build women's leadership for participation in leadership and decision making positions	2.62	1.22
Stereotyping Behavior	Stereotyping is a factor that influences women's participation in the world of work, hence it affects them negatively	2.45	1.47
	Our deep rooted stereo typed behavior is what matters in increasing the women participation in leadership and decision making position.	2.71	1.34
	Generally, it is possible to say that stereotype behavior affect the smooth functioning of women's participation in leadership and decision making position.	2.82	1.32

(Contd...)

Work Place Policies	The work place policies of our office are effective, efficient and strong enough in empowering women to enjoy leadership and decision making position.	2.11	1.23
	The offices principles, regulations, and directions can be a barrier to women's participation in leadership and decision making position.	3.21	1.34
	After all one can judge that policies of working place can significantly affect women's participation in leadership and decision making position.	3.11	1.33
Limited access to Advanced Education	You can judge that limited access to advanced education affects women participation in leadership and decision making position in your office.	2.27	1.45
	In adequate training in our office adversely affected female employees to have increased participation in maki.ng effective and efficient decision	2.95	1.26
	I can say that there is not good reputation in training and education for our office regarding empowering women.	1.87	1.12
Discrimination in Appointment	Usually, appointing male employees as a leader and decision maker is obvious.	3.07	1.30
	Discrimination against women can be traced as a major factor for reduced percentage of female employees in the position of Leadership and decision making	2.73	1.35
	There is discrimination against women in appointment for Leadership and decision making position.	3.16	1.32

Source: Own Field Survey, 2019.

In the above table, one can see that the researcher has tried to analyze six factors with three dimensions each. This analysis shows that the highest mean for the dimensions of social factor is 3.04 and standard deviation of almost 1 with minor deviation from the possible mean value of the total mean in the distribution. Likewise, organizational factor dimensions earned the highest mean score of 2.81 and the average distribution of scores around the mean approaches to 1 that directly reflects the response rate was consistent and respondents were similar in their view on the issue.

In addition, regarding the dimensions of the stereotyping behavior, the highest mean value earned was 2.82 and standard deviation of 1.32 while the dimension for the work place condition earned the highest mean value of 3.21 with standard deviation of 1.34. Regarding the dimensions for the limited access to advanced education, the highest mean value was 2.95 with a standard deviation of 1.26. in the same tale, it was shown that the highest mean value for the dimensions of the "discrimination in Appointment" was 3.16 with standard deviation of 1.32.

From the above (Table 4.9), one can understand that though the general response shows that each major variable employed to measure the concept earned mean value greater than the possible mean (mean value of 2.5) still the result persists that it was below the highest possible mean value that would have been mean value of 5 if things had been fully right.

In our case, discrimination in appointment, work place policies and organizational factors greatly affect the potential of women to come to the position specially regarding participating in deciding on the issue of personal, economic, social political and cultural aspects.

4.5.1 Composite Scores for Factors Affecting Women's' Participation in Leadership and Decision Making Position

For the purpose of simplicity and understandability of the analysis, the researcher has compiled each item under each major dimension together so as to get a compiled result that enables to present and discus these major variables as per specific objective of the study. Table 4.10 below shows composite mean and standard deviation used to measure the major variables.

Table 4.10. Composite Mean Score for Factors Affecting Women's Participation in Leadership and Decision Making Position.

No	*Variables*	*Mean*	*SD*
1.	Discrimination in Appointment	2.98	1.32
2.	Work Place Policies	2.81	1.30
3.	Organizational Culture	2.74	1.31
4.	Stereotyping Behavior	2.66	1.37
5.	Social /cultural Factors	2.65	1.20
6.	Limited Access to Advanced education	2.36	1.27

Source: Own Field Survey, 2019.

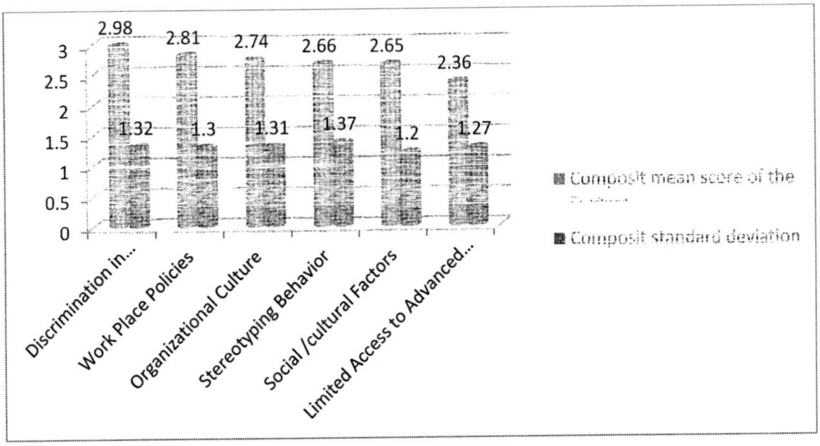

Source: Own Field Survey, 2019.

Figure 4.1: Mean Score and Standard Deviation for Factors Affecting Women's Participation in Leadership and Decision Making Positions.

The above Table 4.10 and Figure 1 reveals that the Discrimination in Appointment factor earned a composite mean value of 2.98 with composite standard deviation of 1.32 while Work Place Policies got the composite mean value of 2.81 with composite standard deviation of 1.30 followed by Organizational Culture dimension with composite mean value of 2.74 and composite standard deviation of 1.31. Likewise, Stereotyping Behavior has earned composite mean value of 2.66 and composite standard deviation of 1.37. In the same figure, it is shown that Social /cultural Factors dimension has earned composite mean value of 2.65 and composite standard deviation of 1.20 followed by Limited Access to Advanced with composite mean value of 2.36 and composite standard deviation of 1.27.

Regarding the above factor, the open ended response revealed that the discrimination in appointment factor (underestimation of females by giving priority to men in appointment which resulted in reduced percentage of female employees in the position of Leadership and decision making) followed by workplace factor that offices principles, regulations, and directions are barrier to women's participation in leadership and decision making position. work place policies are not effective, efficient and strong enough in empowering women to enjoy leadership and decision making position. In addition to this, the inflexible nature of organizational structure greatly affects women's participation in the position of leadership and decision making. Regarding the factors mentioned above, the same result was acquired from th FGD.

The analysis from the composite mean score shows that the discrimination in appointment, work place and organizational culture factors greatly affect the potential of women\s participation in leadership and decision making position.

4.6. Issues on the Management and Leadership Practice (Managerial Function) of the Sub City.

Considering that the managerial functions of a management is vital for all the performance achieved, and then the researcher has assessed and analyzed the level of practice of managerial functions to determine its effectiveness in all cases.

Table 4.11. Management and Leadership Practice of the Intuitions.

Variable	*Statement of the Question*	*Mean*	*SD*
Planning	In my opinion, the office has a proactive, effective and efficient plan to capacitate women for leadership and decision making position	1.99	1.18
Organizing	The office usually tries its best in organizing important activities and resources in the way it enables women to have increased participation in leadership and decision making position	2.02	1.19
Directing (Leading)	How do you understand and judge the way your office is leading (inspiring, motivating, and directing) its employees to increase the overall participation of women in leadership and decision making position	2.48	1.48
Controlling	What is the status of your office's controlling (monitoring and evaluation) of is activities and strategies in relation to bringing women to leadership and decision making positions.	1.95	1.19

Source: Own Field Survey, 2019.

As it is displayed in the above table 4.11, the mean value of planning function of the institution was 1.99 with 1 frequent response and 1.18 standard deviation of distribution of scores around the mean value of the total distribution. In addition the mean value for organizing function was 2.02 with frequent value of 2 (mode of 2) and standard deviation 1.19 that indicates little deviation of scores from the mean value. Likewise the table tells us that the mean score for directing /leading was 2.48 with frequent value of 2 (mode of 2) and standard deviation of 1.48 while the mean value of controlling function was 1.95 with frequent value of 1 and standard deviation of 1.19.

From the analysis, the researcher can understand that all the managerial functions and the area of leadership earned a mean value less than the mean value of 2.5 and for less than the highest possible mean value (mean value of 5). On the other hand, the result shows us that the respondents had similar opinion on the managerial functions of the institution that could be understood from the above results, standard deviation and the lower level (mode 1 &2) in the established scales was the frequent response that was rated by the respondents.

In the case of this study's result under the objective, the management and administration of the public sectors in the area was not giving strong attention in including the issue of gender mainstreaming that if had it been focused, the better mean value would have been scored. Briefly speaking, there was great problem on planning. Organizing, leading and controlling through empowerment and the way that could not be compromised with quality.

4.7. Discussion and Interpretation of the Results

4.7.1. Introduction

In the preceding sections of the study, the data gathered on on each objective of the study were separately presented under different sub topics. Based on the findings, the following sections discuss and synthesize the results in the light of the specific objectives of the study.

4.7.2. Status of Women's Participation in Leadership and Decision Making Position

Table 4.2 has shown that there were less female leaders and greater in proportion of male leaders in decision making positions. It was very visible that greater number of respondents replied that there were even far less number of women in core positions which shows that they were rejected /marginalized from potentially access to decision making and leading the communities and developing themselves.

To bring about the change in the public sector, the role of management as a whole is so vital if they are to realize the fact that women are on integral part-taker of different personal, social, economical, cultural and political issue of a given country in general and a given organization in particular. To confirm the idea still the number of women employees were great in number in position that were rated as inferior positions like cleaner. This has further reflection of women's marginalization that seek overwhelming action from all including female themselves.

According to Philips, (2003) women constitute almost 50% of the world's population that makes their development and level of productivity vital to the nation economic development. However, due to different factors, their participation and contribution have been remained below.

From the analysis regarding the current status of women's participation in leadership and decision making position, one can understand that majority of female employees were relatively in lower and non decision making position. To confirm this more, the reflection in terms of participation of employees in other job title like cleaners holds more female employees as compared to males in the sampled sectors. Even though women bear the burden of almbhost every activity related to reproduction and are equally active as their male counter parts in the field of production and community work, the patriarchal system do not allow them in most cases to be owners of resource (Hirut, 2004). In similar manner, Panos, (2005) women are not also given opportunity to make decisions by their own even on the matters related to their personal life. This idea has been supported by the finding of this study that in most cases women are marginalize from participating in leadership and decision making positions.

4.7.3. Attitudes and Awareness of Women and their Male Counter Parts About Women's Competency in Leadership and Decision Making Position

The interview result from the majority of the respondents had the reflection that even females demoralize themselves by relating the case to different spots like; inability to take responsibility and rushing from being risk taker. This seeks some sort of ways from the management side, to improve the capacity of women and men to change their attitudes and realize the importance of women's contribution and roles in any development program and decision making from agenda setting to policy development.

This is because it is inevitable for the government or any entity to share its resources to women and benefit from their engagement and success if inclusive development is expected to realize through development of different initiatives.

4.7.4. Perception of women's and their Male Counter Parts towards Women's Assertiveness in Leadership and Decision Making Position

Table 4.4. shows that there is no significant difference between male and female with respect to the items used to measure the perception of women and their male counterparts towards women's assertiveness in leadership and decision making position. This can, for example, be understood from the item (dimension) " women have sound mind as men have" which is rated by both female and male respondents that is female (Mean = 3.34, SD = 1.17) and male (Mean = 3.31, SD = 1.12).

From the analysis one can understand that the response from both female and male on the variables used to measure the concept of "assertiveness" dimension has statistically insignificant difference.

On the other hand, there was a focus group discussion which shows that there is significant difference between female and male in assertiveness that is the concept used to reflect to what extent female are standing for their right in a convincing manner in respect to their male counter parts.

This could be understood especially from the groups' explanation of " men are usually more assertive than women" that directly affects their participation in the position of leadership and decision making. The other important idea raised in the FGD was that the female discourage themselves believing that they are less assertive regarding standing for one's own right and benefit.

According to Ishetu, (2004) the values in which we developed affects to what extent one stands for her/his right in assertive way that this statement is directly related to our case. These values and behaviors usually come to dominate females in their organizations and their lives including their degree of participation in different activities.

Furthermore, the interview response confirm the same ideas that underestimates potentiality of women stating that there is significant difference between male and female respondents regarding the assertiveness issues that could be understood from the reflection of their ideas in such a way that male are usually convincing in their assertion and their judgment in every public and private issues whether it is economic or social issues.

Thus, the general analysis of the study on the concept allows us to understand that there was a seemingly difference between the objective response and the open discussion and interviews. This can evoke us to take decisions like there is problem regarding assertiveness dimension that underestimate females.

4.7.5. Attitudes of Women's and their Counterparts towards Women's Confidence in Leadership and Decision Making Position.

The analysis in table 4.5. Shows that there is no significant difference between the response of female and male respondents towards women's confidence in leadership and decision making position. For instance, the result of the respondents in the table regarding the item 'Women can reason out their point of view" , female (Mean = 1.41, SD = .494) and male (Mean = 1.44, SD = .594) tells us that there is no statistical significant difference in mean on the normal distribution.

From the analysis, one can understand that the difference between the response of male and female on the variables used to measure the concept of "confidence" dimension is statistically insignificant.

According to Powell, (2002) many Kenyan women work hard but the authorities in charge of promotion do not recognize them. Lawsakily. et.al (2004) argues that unlike our male counterparts, who will be asked for monetary favors in appointments, women are under pressure to give sexual favors. From our analysis, it is possible to deduce that similar problems in other African countries are facing our females.

The FGD response tells us that there is significant difference between male and female in confidence dimension that is the concept used to reflect to what extent female are confident in their action, decision making and leadership activities relative to to their male counterparts. This could be understood especially from the group's explanation of women are usually less confident than their male counterparts that directly affects their participation in the position of leadership and decision making in many aspects.

The other important idea raised by the FGD, regarding this issue, was that females discourage themselves believing that they are less confident in accomplishing their responsibilities to the standard they are expected.

Furthermore the interview response reveals that there is significant difference between male and female respondents regarding the confidence issues. According to the interview response from the majority of the respondents, "women are less confidence than men in their decision making position and their counterpart male are more confident in all aspects. The interview respondents said that female underestimate themselves that directly impact heir lives even beyond their participation in leadership and decision making position.

The general analysis of the study on the confidence concept allows us to understand that male parts of the respondents persist that women are less confident than their male counterparts. The other major idea they raised regarding this issue is that in judging their own issue women seek men's support and also they reflected that men can decide on women's and men's issues and agendas in an independent manner.

4.7.6. Perception of Women and their Male Counterparts Towards Women in Leadership and Decision Making Position

The analysis of the finding tends to reveal that there is statistically slight difference between male and female perception of women's and their male counterparts towards women in leadership and decision making position. This can for example be justified from item No. 4 in table 4.6 that is "men and women can equally shoulder equal weight of responsibility" the response of female and male respondents which show, female (Mean = 1.63, SD =0.72) and male (Mean = 1.62, SD =0.70).

From the analysis, it is possible to deduce that females are arguing that they have the perception that they are capable of occupying leadership and decision making position regardless of the underestimating perception of their counterparts. This shows us that women are more optimistic about themselves than the attitude that males hold about the female' potential of occupying the positions that have negative connotations. Similarly Panos, (2005) stresses that male's attitude towards women is non motivating relative to their counterparts women and this further supports te finding of this study. It is also possible to deduce from the study that in almost all the variables of measurement of "perception" men's perception/ attitude discourages women from participating in leadership and decision making position and beyond this, it affects women's actual role in deciding on their personal and social issues and benefits. According to Mekuria et. al, (2005) in any ethnic group in Africa a typical woman has low status particularly lack of power to make decisions on matters affecting her life and those of her family. This culturally determined expectation and attitude towards the girl child influences less allocation of resources towards the girl as compared to the boys. A boy will always be considered first before a girl. Thus this source reassures the finding of this study showing spots on African countries among which our country Ethiopia is one.

According to the focus groups' ideas reflections, men hold attitudes with negative connotations towards their counter parts women. The average response from the focus group has the tendency to hold the idea that men are pessimistic about women's capability and relatively women are more optimistic about themselves regarding their ability and potential to occupy leadership and decision making positions.

Furthermore, the interview response reveals that there is significant difference between male and female respondents regarding the perception dimension. According to the interview response from the majority of the respondents, women are more optimistic than men in occupying leadership and decision making positions while their counterpart men are more pessimistic than women almost in all aspects.

4.7.7 Awareness of Women and their Male Counter Parts About Women's Competency in Leadership and Decision Making Position.

The result shown on table 4.7 reveals that there is statistically slight difference between the response of male and female respondents with respect to awareness of women and their male counter parts about women's competency in leadership and decision making position. For example, there is statistically slight difference between male and female revealed by the result of female and male respondents with respect to the item "The employees of your office are flexible enough in solving gender related problems", female (mean = 2.88, SD = 1.2) and male (mean = 2.74, SD = 1.2).

From the analysis, one can infer that the response from both male and female on the variables used to measure the awareness level of the respondents is statistically significant. The analysis shows that the response of both women and their men counter parts tends to be balance indicating that both men and women do not have significant difference in their level of awareness on the issues reflecting level of participation of women in leadership and decision making positions. According to the reflection of focus group's ideas, women are more likely to recognize the importance and openness of women to change than their men counter parts. The average response from the FGD has the tendency to hold the idea that men are with less awareness and more pessimistic about the importance of women's capability in making decision and being in leadership position. Furthermore, the interview response reveals that there is statistically slight difference between male and female respondents regarding recognizing the importance and readiness of women in leadership position and decision making. According to the interview response from the majority of the respondents, "women women are more aware of their importance in leadership and decision making positions than their men counterpart almost in all aspects.

According to (Meaza ,2009), the level of social awareness and its culture is often used as a tool to validate all members of actions –not, all of which may be acceptable to all concerned -and are often intimately, connected to issues of identity. In similar sense, cultural frameworks are not always imposed, but are open to manipulation and interpretation from many angles and sources Hayot, (2005). Here the finding and the statement of the authors confirm each other reflecting that the problem is wide spread.

If we combine the value of the analysis, one can understand that women and their counter parts men are not induced with internalized awareness that can influence them to recognize the importance of women's participation in leadership and decision making positions.

4.7.8. Contribution of the existing Policy Framework in Encouraging Women's Participation in Leadership and Decision Making Position.

The professional understanding of the researcher can forward that the average response rate for all the variables used to measure the nature of the existing policy framework in different dimensions earned the average value of less than the highest possible mean value. Furthermore, all the variables employed to measure the objective did not earn the value on the scale greater than 2 that reveals the respondents' view of the policy framework inefficiency and that there is problem with policy framework. In other words, the respondents' response was so consistent and concentrated in their distribution around the average score that provide further understanding of similarity of respondents' view towards the nature of the existing policy framework.

According to a policy formulated by the existing Ethiopian Government (FDRE, 1995) a policy is expected to play a significant role in facilitating conditions to speed up of equality between men and women in order to let women participate in the social, economic and political life their country in equal terms with that of men and women's roles and participation in decision making positions and their enjoyment of their fruits and benefits of development on equal basis with men were emphasized in the content of the national policy (FDRE, 1995). Therefore, based on this FDRE policy point of view, the respondents' response on our context reflected that there is slight problem with some aspects of the policy and the main problem with implementation of the policy indeed. The policy practicability is vital for the success of an organization that it can aid in making the whole processes and mechanisms formal and consistent in its proceedings. In relation to this idea, some of the interview respondents had the idea to reflect that though the policy is supportive in nature, yet it was still demanding great attention and commitment from the management through implementation of different policy instruments/ tools and directives that are practical and cost effective in their nature. In line with this idea, the focus group discussion result generated a detail and corporate idea that stresses the nature of the existing policy frame work on the area of bringing women to the leadership and decision making position, to some extent, has strong side specially regarding giving insights to both sexes on the importance of women's participation not only in leadership and decision making position, but also in any activity that directly or indirectly affects their social, economical, personal and political issues. In other words, the FGD forwarded that still there were a number of problems in implementation of the existing policy because of different bias, incompetency, and uncommitted nature of civil servants that made the policy passive and corrupt.

The systems of the literature and the findings of this study confirm each other in such a way that a policy like in our case the policy that encourages women to the position of leadership and decision making should be clear, content specific, comprehensive, sound, practicable, problem solving and supportive in nature.

4.7.9. Examining which Factor(s) Significantly Affect the Women's Participation in leadership and Decision Making Position

A management of an organization that runs a resource and community should continuously update itself so that it can stay in the competitive environment and use its human resource executively and efficiently. In the case of this study, as can be seen from the above Table 4.10, one can understand that though the general response shows that each major variable employed to measure the factors that significantly affect the level of women's participation in the leadership and decision making position earned mean value of greater than the possible mean value of 2.5, still the result persists that it was below the highest value that would have been value of 5 if things had been fully right.

Therefore, the issue requires managerial attention and commitment since the effective and efficient management of these factors lead to improved participation of women in leadership and decision making position. In addition, the management should give attention to these factors that may greatly affect their level of participation in leadership and decision making position. In our case discrimination in appointment and work place policies greatly affect the potential of women to come to the position especially regarding participating in deciding on the issues of personal, economic, social, political and cultural aspects. According to Meaza (2009), the main factors that have contributed for disparities between male and female participation in leadership and decision making position include; structural barriers, unequal socio-economic opportunities and inadequate access to mentors and support networks. Furthermore, the same source has depicted out that rigid work place structure and greater stereotypes that relate socially defined characteristics with certain groups in most cases also dissociate women from leadership roles.

Similar to the above idea, the interview response confirms that among other factors, the organizational and work place factors greatly affect and influence women's potential even starting from developing the interest to be in that critical position. Likewise, the FGD response asserts that rather than other factors, the one that affects women's participation in decision making position is the work place factors like relation and a biased way of behaving deviating from the formal way of empowering or encouraging them to participate. According to Panos, (2005) women are the core of the family and household work longer hours than men in nearly every country and do more of the total works than men do, and they contribute more to the development of societies. Despite their notable number and contribution to the development of the society at large, they have not been enjoying the fruits of development equally with their male counter parts due to multifaceted gender based problems they face like the opportunity they are offered in every development endeavour including access to and control over resources compared to men are insignificant.

The analysis from the composite mean score on the factors affecting the participation of the women in the position of leadership and decision making shows that the discrimination in appointment, work place policies and organizational factors, among other factors, affect the potential of women's participation in leadership and decision making position. This finding confirms the above cited authors' views in one way or another. Thus the management of the sub city is expected to give attention to underlying stimulus/ factors if better condition in the area is to be realized.

4.7.10. Issues on the Management and Leadership Practice (Managerial Function) of the Sub City.

The Management and Leadership Practice of the sub city was analized in terms of the four functions of management (Planning, Organizing, Directing and controlling).

From the analysis (in table 4.11), the researcher can understand that all the managerial functions and the area of leadership earned a mean value less than the mean value of 2.5 and for less than the highest possible mean value (mean value of 5). On the other hand, the result shows us that the respondents had similar opinion on the managerial functions of the sub city.

When we see the result of this study in relation to the objective, the management and administration of the public sectors in the sub city was not giving strong attention including the issue of gender mainstreaming that, had it been focused, the better mean value would have been scored. Briefly speaking, there was great problem on planning. Organizing, leading and controlling through women empowerment and the way that could not be compromised with quality.

Chapter Five

Summary, Conclusoins and Recommendations

5.1. Introduction

The summary, conclusions and recommendations of this study are drawn from the key findings by assessing the data obtained from primary and secondary source in order to find out the factors affecting the participation of women in managerial position in Bole Sub City.

In chapter four the data have been analyzed and presented through the use of descriptive statistical tools and then discussed in a more detail. In that chapter, the researcher attempted to answer the basic questions of the research hence the result of the study was synthesized with research works done by others on similar topics and the concepts used in the literature review part of the research was considered in aligning the discussion along with important points that guide the entire process. Based on the major findings, presented above the following summary, conclusions and recommendations are drawn

5.2. Summary of the Finding

The study has started with the assessment of the current status of women's participation in leadership and decision making position under which, the condition how leaders come to their position was assessed. Assessment on the attitudes (assertion, confidence, perception, and awareness) of women and men towards women's participation in leadership and decision making positions was also made. Then, an assessment about how the existing policy framework is designed to encourage participation in leadership and decision making position followed by the assessment of factors affecting women's participation in leadership and decision making position was made. Finally, the effectiveness of the management practice, i.e. the four management functions (planning, organizing, directing and controlling) in the success of every activity was assessed.

The findings of the above mention assessments, based on their sequence in chapter four, are summarized as follows.

5.2.1. Current Status of Women's Participation in Leadership and Decision Making Position

Out of the total number of employees (290) in the selected sectors of the sub city, 149 (53.4%) are female. But, the number of women assigned in leadership and decision making position is smaller than men. This is shown in table 4.2 that male being 46.6% of the total employees in the selected sectors, have occupied 75% of the office heads and 71% of the process owner position while women have occupied only 25% of the office head and 29 % of process owner positions. On the other hand, more women are assigned to the positions which are considered as inferior (non decision making and low income generating positions. This can be justified by the fact that 53% of the expert's position and 100% of other supportive posts like cleaner are are occupied by women.

From the analysis, it can be understood that one of the reasons why women's participation in leadership and decision making position is that the way how leaders come to their position is not merit based rather, it was through network and special relation which marginalizes women.

5.2.2. *Attitudes and Awareness of Women and Men About Women's Competency in Leadership and Decision Making*

Attitudes and Awareness of Women and Men About Women's Competency in Leadership and Decision Making position was tested using four dimensions i.e Assertiveness, Confidence, Perception and Awareness which are presented hereunder.

5.2.2.1. *Assertiveness*

The analysis tells us that the response from both female and male on the variables used to measure assertiveness that is the concept used to reflect to what extent female are standing for their right in a convincing manner in respect to their male counterpart has statistically insignificant difference. On the other hand, there was a focus group discussion (FGD) which shows that there is significant difference between female and male in the issue mentioned above. In the FGD, it was also raised that female discourage themselves that they are less assertive than men regarding standing for their own right and benefit. There was also an interview which confirmed the same ideas that underestimates of women.

The integrated analysis shows that, the less nature of women's assertiveness seems to underestimate and influence the degree of participation of women in leadership and decision making positions.

5.2.2.2. *Confidence*

The analysis in table 4.5 shows that there is no significant difference between the response of female and male respondents towards women's confidence in leadership and decision making position. From the analysis, one can understand that the difference between the response of male and female on the variables used to measure the concept of "confidence" dimension is statistically insignificant.

The FGD response tells us that there is significant difference between male and female in confidence dimension that is the concept used to reflect to what extent female are confident in their action, decision making and leadership activities relative to their male counterparts.

The other important idea raised by the FGD, regarding this issue, was that females discourage themselves that they are less confident in accomplishing their responsibilities to the standard they are expected.

Furthermore the interview response reveals that there is significant difference between male and female respondents regarding the confidence issues. According to the interview response from the majority of the respondents, "women are less confidence than men in their decision making position and their counterpart male are more confident in all aspects. The interview respondents said that female underestimate themselves that directly impact their lives even beyond their participation in leadership and decision making position.

The general analysis of the study on the confidence concept allows us to understand that male parts of the respondents persist that women are less confident than their male counterparts. The other major idea they raised regarding this issue is that in judging their own issue women seek men's support and also they reflected that men can decide on women's and men's issues and agendas in an independent manner.

5.2.2.3. Perception

The analysis of the finding tends to reveal that there is statistically slight difference between male and female perception of women's and their male counterparts towards women in leadership and decision making position.

From the analysis, it is possible to deduce that females have the perception that they are capable of occupying leadership and decision making position regardless of the underestimating perception of their counterparts. According to the focus groups' ideas reflections, men hold attitudes with negative connotations towards their counter parts women. The average response from the focus group has the tendency to hold the idea that men are pessimistic about women's capability and relatively women are more optimistic about themselves regarding their ability and potential to occupy leadership and decision making positions.

Furthermore, the interview response reveals that there is significant difference between male and female respondents regarding the perception dimension. According to the interview response from the majority of the respondents, women are more optimistic than men in occupying leadership and decision making positions while their counterpart men are more pessimistic than women almost in all aspects.

The analysis of the findings tends to reveal that there is statistically slight difference between male and female perception of women's and their male counter parts towards women's in leadership and decision making position.

5.2.2.4. Awareness

The result shown on table 4.7 reveals that there is statistically slight difference between the response of male and female respondents with respect to awareness of women and their male counter parts about women's competency in leadership and decision making position. The analysis shows that the response of both women and their men counter parts tends to be balanced indicating that both men and women do not have significant difference in their level of awareness on the issues reflecting level of participation of women in leadership and decision making positions. The average response from the FGD has the tendency to hold the idea that men are with less awareness and more pessimistic about the importance of women's capability in making decision and being in leadership position.

According to the interview response from the majority of the respondents, "women are more aware of their importance in leadership and decision making positions than their men counterpart almost in all aspects.

If we combine the value of the analysis, one can understand that women and their counter parts men are not induced with internalized awareness that can influence them to recognize the importance of women's participation in leadership and decision making positions.

5.2.3. Contribution of the Existing Policy Framework in Encouraging Women's Participation in Leadership and Decision Making Position

The professional understanding of the researcher can forward that the average response rate for all the variables used to measure the nature of the existing policy framework in different dimensions earned the average value of less than the highest possible mean value. Furthermore, the respondents' response was so consistent and concentrated in their distribution around the average score that provide further understanding of similarity of respondents' view towards the nature of the existing policy framework.

Based on the FDRE policy point of view, the respondents' response on our context reflected that there is slight problem with some aspects of the policy and the main problem with implementation of the policy indeed. The policy practicability is vital for the success of an organization that it can aid in making the whole processes and mechanisms formal and consistent in its proceedings. In relation to this idea, some of the interview respondents had the idea to reflect that though the policy is supportive in nature, yet it was still demanding great attention and commitment from the management through implementation of different policy instruments/ tools and directives that are practical and cost effective in their nature.

In line with this idea, the focus group discussion result generated a detail and corporate idea that stresses the nature of the existing policy frame work on the area of bringing women to the leadership and decision making position, to some extent, has strong side specially regarding giving insights to both sexes on the importance of women's participation not only in leadership and decision making position, but also in any activity that directly or indirectly affects their social, economical, personal and political issues. In other words, the FGD forwarded that still there were a number of problems in implementation of the existing policy because of different bias, incompetency, and uncommitted nature of civil servants that made the policy passive and corrupt.

5.2.4. Factors the Significantly Affect Women's Participation in Leadership and Decision Making

A management of an organization that runs a resource and community should continuously update itself so that it can stay in the competitive environment and use its human resource executively and efficiently. In the case of this study, as can be seen from Table 4.10, one can understand that though the general response shows that each major variable employed to measure the factors that significantly affect the level of women's participation in the leadership and decision making position earned mean value of greater than the possible mean value of 2.5, still the result persists that it was below the highest value that would have been value of 5 if things had been fully right.

From the analysis, the major factors that affect women leadership and decision making in the offices were identified. The analysis from the composite mean score on the factors affecting the participation of the women in the position of leadership and decision making shows that the discrimination in appointment, work place policies and organizational factors, among other factors, affect the potential of women's participation in leadership and decision making position.

Accordingly, discrimination in appointment and work place policies followed by organizational culture greatly affect the potential of women to come to the position especially regarding participating in deciding on the issues of personal, economic, social, political and cultural aspects. Furthermore, the same source has depicted out that stereotype behavior that relate socially defined characteristics with certain groups in most cases also dissociate women from leadership roles.

Similar to the above idea, the interview response confirms that among other factors, the organizational and work place factors greatly affect and influence women's potential even starting from developing the interest to be in that critical position. Likewise, the FGd response asserts that rather than other factors, the one that affects women's participation in decision making position is the work place factors like relation and a biased way of behaving deviating from the formal way of empowering or encouraging them to participate. Despite their notable number and contribution to the development of the society at large, they have not been enjoying the fruits of development equally with their male counter parts due to multifaceted gender based problems they face like the opportunity they are offered in every development endeavour including access to and control over resources compared to men are insignificant.

5.2.5. Issues on the Management and Leadership Practice (Managerial Function) of the Sub City.

The Management and Leadership Practice of the sub city was analized in terms of the four functions of management (Planning, Organizing, Directing and controlling).

When we see the result of this study in relation to the objective, the management and administration of the public sectors in the sub city was not giving strong attention including the issue of gender mainstreaming that, had it been focused, the better mean value would have been scored. Briefly speaking, there was great problem on management functions through women's empowerment and the way that could not be compromised with quality.

5.3. Conclusion

The study has tried to assess the current status of women's participation in leadership and decision making position, the attitudes of women and men towards women's participation in leadership and decision making positions, how the existing policy framework is designed to encourage participation in leadership and decision making position, factors affecting women's participation in leadership and decision making position and the effectiveness of the management practice in the success of every activity in the public sectors of Bole sub city.

On the basis of the assessment, the major findings of the study have been outlined and forwarded below as a conclusion.

The study shows that, currently women are under-represented in leadership and decision making roles, where important decisions that affect their lives are taken. From the analysis, it can be understood that one of the reasons why women's participation in leadership and decision making position is that the way how leaders come to their position is not merit based rather, it was through network and special relation which marginalizes women.

The assessment of the attitude of women and men towards the capability of women to carry responsibility tells us that women and their counter parts men are not induced with internalized awareness that can influence them to recognize the importance of women's participation in leadership and decision making positions.

The government of Ethiopia has set out an enabling environment by issuing a national policy on women which is intended, among others, to bring equal participation of women and men in the economic, social and political life of the country. The FDRE constitution government has also included women's rights in the constitution. But, according to this study's finding, there are problems in implementation of this policy in relation to its comprehensiveness, clear indicators for monitoring and evaluation, pro-activeness and problem solving. In Bole Sub City selected sector offices there is still lack of participation of women in leadership and decision making position in relation to their counter parts, male. The affirmative action that women are entitled to in the constitution still awaits implementation mainly in the political sphere.

From the analysis, the major factors that affect women leadership and decision making in the offices were identified. The analysis from the composite mean score on the factors shows us that the discrimination in appointment, work place policies and organizational factors, among other factors, affect the potential of women's participation in leadership and decision making position.

In general, so many factors contributing to gender equality are addressed by the government but still women are under-represented in organizations and in key areas of development as well as in the community affairs and in matters concerning their lives and those of their children. Women who constitute half of the population of the sub city, while performing many important productive, reproductive and community works are also major actors in development.

5.4. Recommendations

Based on the major findings of the study, the followings recommendations are submitted for implementation by the respective stakeholders. Implementation of all recommendations is necessary to reduce the existing gap and improve the imbalance of women in leadership and decision making positions.

- The sub city should give great emphasis to bring women in leadership and decision making position because women's empowerment is a human right issue that lies at the heart of development and the achievement of the MDGs. In addition to this, there are no clear criteria while assigning of managerial positions in the sub city. So the sub city should state the criteria clearly for all employees, thus every staff can have awareness about the criteria and able to compete with confidence.
- Efforts to increase the number of women leaders and decision makers should be encouraged and get supported like through practice of affirmative action for women at the sub city levels. In other words, the management of the sub city should ensure the equality of women with men in all its organizations without compromising with quality.

- The Government of the sub city should also monitor and evaluate the implementation of gender equality principles in staff recruitment, promotion, training, transfer and mechanisms for enforcement of constitutional rights related to the reproduction of female employees and establish system to control the implementation, advocate and lobby for implementation affirmative action which has been provided for in the constitution and take action for those who do not implement it.
- Transparency and meritocracy should be the only criteria to be used when making appointments and promotions in both private and public sectors. Merit based assignment should be maintained at leadership level and women should be provided with opportunities based on their competence and merit.
- The use of network as a means of getting promoted or recruited should be minimized if not eliminated.
- Though there was a sort of participation of female employees in the leadership and decision making position, it requires strict attention from management and concerned bodies.
- Not only giving attention to the quantity of women but also the way they come to the leadership and decision making position should be considered and it should be through transparent ways and a sort of merit based selection. This avoids the manifestation of bias and encourages a sense of competition among women and their counterpart men group/employees.
- Training programs for women's leadership skills should be in place based on the continuous performance measurement.

- The women and youth office of the sub city should encourage the wide spread of research on the areas that target to benefit women through building the competencies and confidence of women.
- Any charity and NGOs in the sub city should include this issue to their priority in their development programs and projects.
- The administrative bodies of the sub city should work collaboratively with other internal and external stakeholders to increase confidence of female through different education, training, promotion opportunities.
- In parallel to capacitating women efforts to change the attitudes of men is so critical for the success of the development projects and programs that are aimed to benefit women.
- Women themselves should analyze between the fact and the groundless attitudes that simply underestimate their potential to lead and decide.
- The administration of the sub city in general and women affairs bureau and NGOs in particular should work hard to change the attitude of society concerning the deep rooted cultural perceptions of women as inferior to men which has been and continued to be major hindrance to women's advancement in the area of power sharing and decision making through arranging intensive training, awareness raising forums by using different media and community social structure and facilitating different experience sharing for women leaders from abroad.
- The management of the sub city should capacitate the institutional mechanism for the advancement of

women affairs offices at different levels with qualified leaders and financial resources in order to realize the implementation of international and national policies on women.

- The public sectors/ government should also create gender friendly organization culture and foster a working environment of mutual respect between male and female employees, avoid stereotyping and discrimination of work place and institute a system of incentive/ motivation for positive attitude and work that reflect gender sensitive image for work sections and offices.
- The existing policy should be revised in a way that enables implementation with less cost and effort.
- The government of the sub city and other responsible bodies should support financially the expansion of appropriate technological devices which could save women labor time and relieve their burdensome chores/ house hold jobs/ and allow them time to be engaged in other productive activities like participating in leadership and decision making positions.
- The government in general and the management of the sub city in particular should work towards the reduction of the impact of work place policies and organizational factors which have been identified as the major one in this study.
- Therefore, the issue requires managerial attention and commitment since the effective and efficient management of these factors lead to improved participation of women in leadership and decision making position.

- The management should give attention to the factors that may greatly affect women's level of perception in leadership and decision making position.
- The management (administration) of the sub city is expected to give attention to these underlying factors if better condition in the area is to be realized.
- The decision making bodies of the sub city should mobilize their efforts and available resources in such a way ensures that women are able to contribute to and benefit from any development program and projects that can directly and/ or indirectly affect their lives and their families.
- Women continue to move in to government organizations and increase their share of professional and leadership positions.
- If not, it would be unrealistic to think of achieving democracy and good governance with such a huge force excluded from leadership positions and decision making process.

Bibliography

Afroz, M. (2010). *Effect of Organizational Governance on Women's Participation in Decision Making, Master in Public Policy and Governance Program, Department of General and Continuing Education,*. Bangladish: North South University.

Ajack, O. (1992). *Hong Kong Secondary School Women Principales: Study of Gender Bias. The University of Hong Kong.* Hong Kong.

Amrot, T. (1998). *The Participation Ethiopian Women in the Profession and Practice of Management. A Case of Commercial Bank of Ethiopia, Ethiopian Airlines, Ministry of Transport and Communication and Ministry of Foreign Affairs, In Partial Fulfillment of the Reuirement fo.* Addis Ababa.

Azeb, F. (2003). *Ethiopian Women the Public Sphe, their Role and Predicament, B.A Thesis.* A.A.

Biseswar, I. (2011). *The Role of Educated/Intelectual Women in Ethiopia in the Process of Change and Transformation towards Gender Equality 1974-2005: Submitted in fulfillment of the Reqirement for the Degree of phd in the subject Sociology, University of South Africa* . A.A.

Brenda, N. (2015). *Factors Determining Womens Participation in Decision Making in Zambia revenue Authority.* Zambia: The Universty of Zambia.

Chin. (2007). *Women and Leadership Transforming Vision and Diverse Voice.* Black Well Publishing Ltd.

Collical, H. (2009). *Research Methods and Statstics in Psychology.* . London: By Hodder Education, an Hachette UK Company. 33 B Easton Road, London NW 13 B 4.

Commission, E. (2010). *EU Plan of action in Gender Equality and Women's Impowerment and Development: Commission Staff Documents 2010-2015.*

CSA. (2007). *Summary and Statstics Report 2007 Population and Housing Censes, Population Size by Age and Sex.* A.A.

D., H. (2009). *Empowerment of Women in Decision Making: Institute of Public Management and Development Studies, Ethiopian Civil Service University.* A.A.

DHS, E. s. (2005). *Gender Inequality and Womens empowerement* . A A.

EC. (2010). *European Commission , (2010) EU Plan of Action in Gender Equality and Women's Impowerment and development: Commission Staff Documents-2010-2015.*

Elsi, L. (2013). *Women and Leadership: Factors that Influence Women's Career Success. Female Leaders' Reflections on their Career Development and Leadership, Thesis.* University of Applied Science.

Freeman. (2001). *Women on Power, Leadership Redefine.*

Ginige, K. Amaratunga, D. & Haigh, R. (2007). *Gender Stereotypes: A Barrier for Career Development of Women in Construction.* Salford: University of Salford.

Growe, R. & Montgomery, P. (2000). "Women and the Leadership Paradigm: Bridging the Gender Gap." National Forum. *The Phikappa Phi Journal* , 17, 1-10.

Haregewoin. (2009). *Empowerment of Women in Decision Making: Institute of Public Management and Development Studies, Ethiopian Civil Service University.* A.A.

Hess C. (2002). *Gender Gap, Women and Education Lan Caster.* Lan Caster: University of Lan Caster.

Israel, D. (2009). *Determining Sample Size.* Florida: IFAS, University of Florida, edis, Ifas, UFL.

Jackson, W. (2003). *Methods: Doing Social Research. Third Edition.* Canada: Prentice Hall.

Kothari, C. (2004). *Research Methodology, Methods and Techniques (2nd Edition).* New Delhi: New Age International (P) Limited Publisher.

Mbugua, W. (2007). *An Investigation of Factors Influencing Women Progression to Leadership Positions in Kenya: A case Study of four selected Institutions. A Research Report Submitted in Partial Fufillment of a Degree of Masters in Business Administration, Kenyata University.* Nairobi.

Mckinsey, R., & Company, S. (2009). *Women eaders, A Competitive Edge in and After the crisis Results of Global Survey of allmost 800 business Leaders Conducted.*

Meaza, A. (2009). *Factors Affecting Women's Participation in Politics and Decision Making, MA Thesis.* A.A.

MOWA. (2004). *A National Report on Progress made in the Implementation of the Bejjing Plate Form for Action (Bejjing +10).* A.A: Ethiopian Prime Minister's Office (Women's Affairs Sub Sector).

Perry, E., Davis-Blake and Kulik, . (1994). *Explaining Gender-Based sellection Decisions: A Synthesis of Contextual and Cognitive Approaches.* Academy of Management Review.

Pooter, M. (2009). *South African Women Gaining Large Share of Political Leadership Role.* Charles Mott Foundation.

Robbins, S. (1992). *Essentials in Organzational Behaviour.* City: Prentice-Hall International Editions.

Sikdar ,Arijit & Mitra Sumit . (2008). *An exploration of gender sterotypes in perception and practice of leadership;.* Duba;University of Wollangoing.: Working paper series.

Stelter, N. (2002). Gender Differences in Leadership: Current Social Issues and Future Organizations. . *Journal of Leadership and Organizational Studies 8.4* , 88.

Suad, M. (2015). *Factors Affecting Women's Particupation in Political Leadership. The case Of Dire Dawa Institution.* A.A.

Takabo H. (2010). *Evaluating the Role of the Male Policy Leaders in Ethiopia University of South Africa.*

UNDP. (1995). *http://www.unicef.org.* Retrieved March 27, 2013, from http://www.unicef.org.

UNDP. (1995). *UNDP1995 Plat form for Action and Beijing Declaration,.* New York: United Nations Department of Public Information.

USAID-IQPEP. (2012). *Exploring Policy- Practice Gaps of Female Leaders in the Ethiopian Education System, Submitted to : The Monitoring Evaluation Research Analysis (MERA) Component .* A.A.

Willis, V. (1991). *"Public Life: Women Make aDifference" Expert Group Meeting on Role of Women in Public Life (Vienna, 21-24 May).* New York.

Wudealem, A. (2015). *Assessment of Factors Affecting Women Participation in Leadership in Some sellected Public Organizations. A case of East Gojam Zone.* A.A.

Yalem, S. (2011). *women in Leader ship and Decision Making in Developmental Organizations;A case of Ethiopian Telecommunications Corporation.* Addis Ababa.: International leadership Institute and University of Greenwich.

Yukl, G. (2006). *Leadership in organization 6 th ed.* Upper saddle river,NJ: pearson- prentice Hall.

List of Abbreviations

A.A	=	Addis Ababa
BDPA	=	Beijing Declaration and Platform of Action
BPFA	=	Beijing Platform for Action
BPR	=	Business Process Re-Engineering
CEDAW	=	Convention on Elimination of all forms of discrimination against women
CSA	=	Central Statistics Agency
E.C	=	European Commission
FGD	=	Focus Group Discussion
IPU	=	Inter-Parliamentarian Union
MDG	=	Millennium Development Goal
MOWA	=	Ministry Of Women Affairs
SD	=	Standard Deviation
SPSS	=	Statistical Package for the Social Sciences
UN	=	United Nations
UNDP	=	United Nations Development Program
WID	=	Women In Development

Index

L

M

N

O

P

Q

R